WARFARE IN THE EIGHTEENTH CENTURY

WARFARE
IN THE
EIGHTEENTH
CENTURY

Jeremy Black

General Editor: John Keegan

CASSELL

For

WARWICK LIGHTFOOT

First published in Great Britain 1999
by Cassell, Wellington House, 125 Strand, London
WC2R 0BB www.cassell.co.uk

British Library Cataloguing-in-publication Data
ISBN: 0-304-352-454

Design: Martin Hendry
Cartography: Arcadia Editions Ltd
Picture research: Elaine Willis

Typeset in Monotype Sabon

Printed in Italy by Printer Trento Srl

ACKNOWLEDGEMENTS

To try to encapsulate a century of conflict and military development in 40,000 words is an exciting challenge. All historical writing involves choice, but at this length the choices are particularly brutal and may lead to the neglect of entire wars and whole countries. I have therefore organized the book in such a way as to make a series of statements. First, that a Eurocentric military history of this period that completely neglects other societies is unacceptable – it is necessary to emphasize that war was a widespread global activity, and that conflicts which did not involve Europeans were important and have much to teach us. Second, in so far as attention is devoted to European military history, much of it should concentrate on the Europeans overseas, both on wars with non-Europeans and on transoceanic conflict with the forces of other European states, as these were most important in global history.

I have benefited greatly from the advice of Matthew Anderson, Gerry Bryant, Jan Glete, Richard Harding, Harald Kleinschmidt, Peter Lorge, Gunther Rothenberg, Armstrong Starkey and Harry Ward, and I would like to thank Penny Gardiner at Cassell for all her help with this book. I am grateful to have had the opportunity to develop themes discussed in this book in lectures delivered at Adelphi, Georgia State, Harvard and Ohio State Universities, at the Universities of Richmond and the West of England, at conferences on Chinese and on South Asian military history at the University of Cambridge, at the Wellington conference at the University of Southampton, at the Dibner Institute conference on Science and Material Culture in Warfare, at the Naval War College in Newport, at the University of Virginia Alumni summer school at Oxford, and at Assumption College. It is a great pleasure to dedicate this study to an old friend.

JEREMY BLACK
Exeter

History of Shah Jahan Muhammad Salih Kanbu. Mughal manuscript.

CONTENTS

KEY TO MAPS

Military units–types

infantry

cavalry

Military unit colours

Military movements

→ attack

⇢ retreat

General military symbols

✕ site of battle

⌂ fort

∿ defensive line

● ● ● skirmish line

⊸ field gun

Geographical symbols

urban area

urban area (3D maps)

river

seasonal river

∙∙∙∙ canal

– – – internal border

—— international border

Map list

CHRONOLOGY

1696 Battle of Gio-modo: the Chinese defeat the Dsungars.

1698 The Omani Arabs take Mombasa from the Portuguese.

1699 The French found a settlement at Biloxi.

1701–14 War of the Spanish Succession (for the British 1702–13).

1704 Aurangzeb storms the Maratha fort of Torna.
Battle of Blenheim: Marlborough's first great victory.

1706 Battle of Ramillies: Marlborough victorious.
Battle of Turin: Austro-Savoyard forces defeat the French.

1707 Battle of Almanza: the French defeat the British.

1708 The Algerians take Oran from Spain.
Battle of Oudenaarde: Marlborough victorious.

1709 Battle of Malplaquet: Marlborough's last and hardest-won victory.
Battle of Poltava: the Russians crush the Swedes.

1710 The French found Mobile.

1711 Battle of the Pruth: Peter the Great surrenders to the Turks.

1715 The Turks conquer the Peloponnese.

1716 Battle of Peterwardein: the Austrians crush the Turks.

1717 The Dsungars invade Tibet and storm Lhasa.
The Spaniards invade Sardinia.
The Venetians hold Corfu against the Turks and take Belgrade.
Battle of Belgrade: the Austrians crush the Turks.

1718 Battle of Cape Passaro: the British defeat the Spanish fleet.

1720 The Chinese conquer Lhasa.

1721 The Ghilzai Afghans invade Persia and capture Kirman.

1722 Battle of Gulnabad: the Ghilzai Afghans defeat the Persians. Isfahan captured.
Russians capture Derbent.

1723 Russians capture Baku.

1723 The Dsungars advance into central Kazakhstan.

1724 Battle of Shakarkhera: Nizam of Hyderabad establishes his position.

Dahomey forces conquer the kingdom of Allada.

1724–5 The Dsungars overrun Turkestan.

1727 Dahomey forces conquer Whydah.

1728 Russo-Chinese Treaty of Kiakhta.

1730 Battle of Nahavand: the Persians under Nadir Kuli defeat the Turks.
The Turkish army rebels.
The French defeat the Fox tribe.

1733–5 War of the Polish Succession.

1733 Battle of Buleleng in Bali.
The French capture Kehl.
Nadir defeats the Turks near Kirkuk.

1734 Battle of Bitonto: the Spanish defeat the Austrians.

1735 Battle of Baghavand: Nadir defeats the Turks.

1736 Nadir Shah conquers southern Afghanistan.
Successful Russian siege of Azov.
Unsuccessful Russian invasion of Crimea.

1737 Successful Russian siege of Ochakov.

Unsuccessful Russian invasion of Crimea.

1738 Nadir Shah captures Kabul and Kandahar.
Battle of Bhopal: the Marathas defeat the Nizam of Hyderabad.
Battle of Talkatora: the Marathas rout the Mughals.
Successful Russian siege of Khotin.

1739 Nadir Shah invades northern India.
Battle of Karnal: Nadir Shah defeats the Mughals.
Nadir Shah captures Delhi.
Belgrade surrendered by the Austrians to the Turks.
Battle of Stavuchanakh: the Russians defeat the Turks.
Admiral Vernon captures Porto Bello.

1740 Nadir Shah conquers the Khanates of Bukhara and Khiva.
Battle of Mollwitz: the Prussians beat Austria.
Battle of Damalcherry: the Marathas defeat the Nawab of the Carnatic.

1740–48 War of the Austrian Succession.

1741–3 Nadir Shah campaigns unsuccessfully in Daghestan.

1741 The British fail to take Cartagena.
Frederick the Great of Prussia invades Silesia.

1741 The Marathas capture Trichinopoly.

1743 Nadir Shah captures Kirkuk.
Battle of Dettingen: the British defeat the French.

1744 Battle of Toulon: indecisive clash between the British and Franco-Spanish fleets.

1745 Battle of Kars: Nadir Shah defeats the Turks.
The British capture Louisbourg.
Battle of Fontenoy: the French under Saxe beat the British.

1746 Battle of Roucoux: the French under Saxe beat the British.

1747 Nadir Shah assassinated.
Battle of Lawfeldt: the French under Saxe beat the British.

1751 The Pimas of Arizona rebel against Spain.

1752 Ahmad Khan of Persia (Iran) annexes Lahore and Kashmir.

1752 Battle of Bhalke: the Marathas defeat the Nizam of Hyderabad.

1755 Battle of the Ili river: the Chinese defeat the Dsungars under Dawaci.

The horse used by the Cheyenne and Pawnee.

1756 Start of the Seven Years War: Frederick the Great invades Saxony.
The French capture Minorca.

1757 Ahmad Khan of Persia annexes Sirhind.
Battle of Rossbach: the Prussians under Frederick the Great defeat the French.
Battle of Leuthen: the Prussians under Frederick the Great defeat the Austrians.
Battle of Plassey: Robert Clive defeats the Nawab of Bengal.
China completes the conquest of Dsungaria.

1757–8 Burma successfully invades Manipur.

1758 The British capture Louisbourg.
Battle of Zorndorf: the Prussians under Frederick the Great beat the Russians.

1759 The Chinese capture Kashgar.
Alaung-hpaya of Burma successfully invades Tenasserim.
The British capture Québec and Niagara.
British naval victories at Lagos and Quiberon Bay.
Battle of Kunersdorf: the Russians beat Prussia.

Battle of Minden: the British beat the French.

1760 The Burmese siege of the Siamese capital of Ayuthia fails.
Battle of Udgir: the Marathas defeat the Nizam of Hyderabad.
Battle of Wandewash: the British under Eyre Coote defeat the French in India.
The British capture Montreal.

1761 Third Battle of Panipat: Ahmad Khan defeats the Marathas.
Haidar Ali seizes power in Mysore.
Kirti Sri of Kandy overruns much of Dutch-held Sri Lanka.

1762 The British capture Havana and Manila from Spain.

1763 The end of the Seven Years War.

1763–4 Pontiac's War.

1764 Battle of P'etchaburi: the Siamese under P'Ya Tashin defeat the Burmese.
The Dutch invasion of Kandy is unsuccessful.
Battles of Patna and Buxar: Victories consolidate the British position in Bengal.

1765 The Burmese invade Manipur.

The Dutch effort to crush Kandy fails.

1766–9 Chinese expeditions against Burma.

1767 Ayuthia stormed by the Burmese. The Siamese king is captured.

1768–74 The Russo-Turkish War.

1769 The Chinese army is trapped by the Burmese under Maha Thi-ha Thu-ra at Kaung-ton.

1770 Battle of Bharatpur: the Marathas defeat the Jats.
Battles of Ryabaya Magila, Larga and Kagul: the Russians defeat the Turks.
Battle of Cesmé: the Russians defeat the Turkish fleet.
The Sioux now using the horse.

1771 Battle of Chinkurali: the Marathas defeat Haidar Ali.

1773 The Burmese attack on Siam fails.

1774 Battle of Kozludji: the Russians defeat the Turks.

1775 Tashin of Siam drives the Burmese from Ching Mai.
Battle of Bunker Hill.

1775–6 The Burmese invasion of Siam.

1776 American Declaration of Independence.

Battle of Long Island: the British defeat the Americans under George Washington.
The British capture New York.
The Persians capture Basra from the Turks.

1777 Battle of Brandywine: the British under Howe defeat the Americans and capture Philadelphia.
Battle of Saratoga: the British are defeated by the Americans.

1778 Tashin of Siam captures Vientiane.
Battle of Ushant: an indecisive British–French naval battle.

1779 Battle of Wadgaon: the British surrender to the Marathas.
A successful Spanish attack on the Comanches.

1780 The British capture Charleston.
Battle of Camden: the British defeat the Americans.

1780–81 Túpac Amaru's rising in Peru.

1781 The British surrender at Yorktown.

1782 Battle of the Saints: the British defeat the French fleet.

1783   Battle of Urai-Ilgasi: the Russians defeat the Nogais.
The end of the War of American Independence.

1784   Bugi siege of Malacca repelled by the Dutch.

1784   The Burmese conquer Arakan.

1785   The Burmese invade Laos and attack Siam unsuccessfully.

1786   The Burmese attack Siam unsuccessfully.

1787   The Turks unsuccessfully besiege rebellious Scutari.
The Tuareg conquer Timbuktu.
Battle of Kinburn: the Russians defeat the Turks.

1788   The Russians storm Ochakov.
Battle of the Dnieper: The Russians defeat the Turkish fleet.

1788–9 The Chinese unsuccessfully attack Tongking (northern Vietnam).

1789   The Austrians take Belgrade.

1790   Darfur captures Kordofan (in modern Sudan).
The Russians capture forts in the Danube delta from the Turks.
The Americans are defeated by the Miamis.

Battle of Tendra: the Russians defeat the Turkish fleet.
Nootka Sound Crisis: the British successfully intimidate the Spaniards.

1791   The British capture Bangalore from Mysore forces, but the advance on Seringapatam fails.
Kamehameha wins dominance of Hawaii.
The Americans are defeated by natives on Wabash river.

1792   The Chinese advance to Katmandu.
The Gurkhas yield.
The British advance successfully on Seringapatam.
Mysore yields.
Battle of Valmy: the French check the Prussians.
Battle of Jemappes: the French defeat the Austrians and overrun Belgium.

1793   The Turks unsuccessfully besiege Scutari.

1794   Battle of Fallen Timbers: the Americans defeat the natives.
The French defeat the Austrians.

1795   The Persians overrun Georgia.

Battle of Nuuanu: Kamehameha is successful in extending power in the Hawaiian chain.
The French overrun the Dutch.

1796   Montenegro successfully resists the Turkish attack.
Napoleon successfully invades northern Italy.

1798   Napoleon invades Egypt.
Nelson defeats the French fleet at the battle of the Nile.

1799   The British capture Seringapatam. Tipu Sultan is killed.

INTRODUCTION

WARFARE IN THE EIGHTEENTH CENTURY

THE BATTLE OF CESMÉ, 5 JULY 1770. The Turkish fleet of twenty ships, the line and frigates and at least thirteen galleys were outmanoeuvred by a smaller Russian squadron off Chios and almost totally destroyed by fireboats. About 11,000 Turks were killed. The Russians, however, failed in their attempt to exploit the situation by driving the Turks from the Aegean.

WARFARE IN THE EIGHTEENTH CENTURY

I N 1757 ALAUNG-HPAYA stormed Pegu, uniting Burma under his rule. In the same year Frederick the Great of Prussia, then fighting what would be known as the Seven Years War (1756–63), defeated his French and Austrian opponents at Rossbach and Leuthen respectively. The latter campaign is frequently cited in works on military history, the former never. Yet both were equally important to contemporaries in their own sphere and to the future development of different regions of the world, and both tell us much that is of interest to the military historian. The same can also be said of campaigns that were less important: for example, the French capture of the fortress of Kehl, the sole gain of their Rhineland advance in 1733 (which would be returned after the 1735 peace), and the major battle at Buleleng in the same year by which Gusti Agung Made Alĕngkajĕng maintained his hegemony in Bali.

The Eurocentric account is limited not only in its coverage, but also in its analysis. The historian assumes that a particular military trajectory, that of the major European powers, is all-important, charts its course and seeks to explain it. By doing so he or she neglects developments in other societies; he or she also fails to offer a comparative account within which European developments can be better appreciated. The Eurocentric approach may appear to be valid when studying 1900, when European states and military methods did indeed dominate most of the world; it is not, however, appropriate for the year 1800, still less so for 1750, when a large part of the world was outside European control.

What then is to be the approach of this book, other than to give an account of warfare in the several parts of the globe? Is there any integrating model?

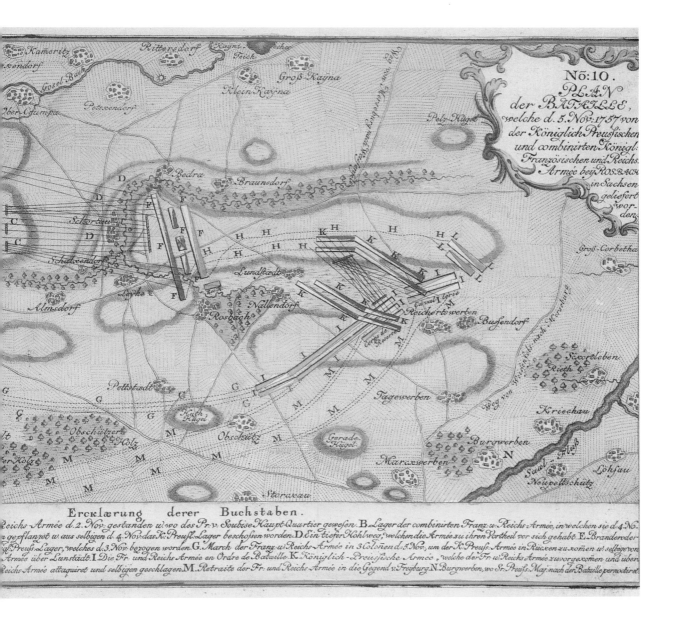

Battle of Rossbach, 5 November 1757. A fast-moving battle in which the speed of the Prussian response under Frederick the Great routed the opposing French army and their German allies. The Prussian infantry fired as it advanced.

First, one theme is, indeed, variety. This is not a matter simply of recording an interesting diversity of military practice, but is, instead, crucial to the argument that different military practices and systems were appropriate in different parts of the world.

Second, and related to the last point, there is no sense of technological triumphalism, no belief that there was a hierarchy of military achievement based on the adoption of particular weapons.

Third, no single model can adequately comprehend both land and naval systems of warfare, and consideration of land and sea underlines the theme of

Battle of Kolin, 18 June 1757. This Prussian defeat badly dented Frederick the Great's reputation. The decision to abandon a planned flank attack and, instead, mount a frontal assault on Daun's well-chosen position led to heavy losses among the Prussian infantry. Frederick's arrogance led him to plan poorly and then to lose control of the battle. The Prussians lost 13,000 men, and abandoned their siege of Prague.

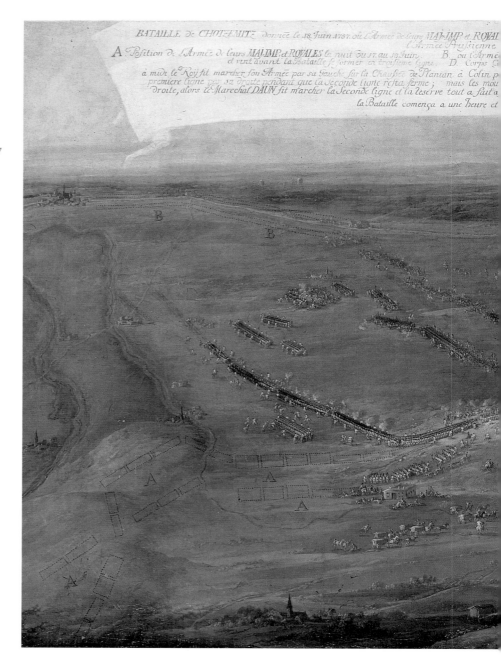

diversity. This theme relates in strategy, tactics and organization to different space/force ratios which can be traced across the globe. In particular, these ratios help account for the continued role of cavalry in many societies. Thus, the standard image of warfare in this period, that of a close-range exchange of fire between tightly-packed lines of infantry – which was, indeed, important in Europe – can be supplemented by a number of others, from the cavalry of central Asia to the Mura archers in their Amazonian fastnesses. In order to illustrate the nature and importance of non-European warfare and also to appreciate what was distinctive about conflict in Europe, I shall begin in Tibet.

In the eighteenth century Asia was the most populous continent of the world, and much of it was little touched by European power. Tibet was the pivot of a struggle between China and its most powerful adversary – not China's European neighbour, Russia, nor the naval powers of western Europe, but the horseman empire of the Dsungars. This struggle indicated that the variety of military methods in the world was a matter of more than variety and curiosity. Different methods reflected the needs of particular military environments. Warfare that did not involve European troops or methods dictated the fate of much of the world in the eighteenth century.

CHAPTER ONE

WAR WITHOUT EUROPEANS

COSSACK RAIDER. Cossacks had a fierce reputation, but were but one example of the light cavalry forces that were so important in eighteenth-century Asia. Such forces combined mobility and fire-power, but made scant impact on fortified positions. The Cossacks became an adjunct of Russian military power.

WAR WITHOUT EUROPEANS

The Kangxi emperor of China (1662–1723) successfully synthesized the Chinese and Manchu military traditions. After suppressing the Rebellion of the Three Feudatories, he expanded Chinese power, defeating the Dsungars in 1696 and 1697.

In 1717 a 6,000-strong Dsungar force invaded Tibet. This expedition, launched by the last of the Mongol nomad empires of central Asia, was, in terms of military techniques, a world away from the Spanish amphibious force that successfully invaded the Mediterranean island of Sardinia in that year. The Dsungar invasion revealed that centuries-old patterns of military behaviour were still valid. Crossing into Tibet by a very high and arid route, the Dsungar horsemen lost many men as a result of the harshness of the terrain, but they pressed on. They had not been sent on a mere raid, which would have been of no consequence except to the victims. On the contrary, the expedition was part of a bitter struggle for mastery over a broad swathe of inner Asia lying between the

Dsungars, based in what is now Xinjiang or north-west China, and the Manchu rulers of China. This struggle lasted until the 1750s and resulted in China expanding to its greatest geographical extent.

Already, in 1696, the Chinese Kangxi emperor had defeated the Dsungar leader Galdan Boshugta at Gio-modo in Mongolia. The two powers had then struggled for dominance in Tibet, which was not then part of China, and control over which would affect the loyalty of the eastern Mongols to China. In 1717 the Dsungar target was Lha-bzan Khan, a Chinese protégé who had deposed the Dalai Lama, the Tibetan spiritual leader, in 1706. Lha-bzan Khan's advisers were divided as to the best way in which to respond to the Dsungars. One, Aka Taiji, recommended fighting in an open plain; another, P'o-lha-nas, suggested taking up a strong defensive position, the strategy adopted by the Chinese in 1696. The former reflected a cultural and social preference for cavalry warfare,

The Kangxi emperor inspecting the building of a dyke. Chinese strength owed much not only to the demographic and economic power of China, but also to the government's ability to mobilize and organize these resources. This was particularly effective in the successful long-distance deployment of forces in Tibet and against the Dsungars.

the latter pressure to use firearms. In the end Lha-bzan's army remained in the pastures that fed his animals, and it was attacked there by the Dsungars. A general musketry volley was followed by fighting at close quarters, particularly with swords and knives, and, after a number of similar battles, Lha-bzan was driven back to Lhasa, which was successfully stormed after midnight on 21 November 1717.

The campaign and its consequences are of wider relevance for students of military history, offering little-known examples of more widespread processes. First, they indicate the transience of military achievement. The Chinese launched a counter-attack in 1718, and, although one Chinese army was wiped out by the Dsungars in that year, concerted operations by two armies led to the conquest of Lhasa two years later. This transience is important because it serves as a reminder of the difficulty of achieving lasting triumphs and of the problems of assessing military capability and effectiveness, both in contemporary terms and over the longer term. Which battles and campaigns are important and worthy of study? How are armies to be judged? The argument that, for example, non-European military systems such as China's were redundant because a century later, at the time of the Opium Wars, they could not resist the Europeans, is unhelpful if it neglects earlier and, at the time, equally testing challenges that did not defeat them.

Chinese swivel gun. Artillery developed differently in China and Europe. The Chinese were aware that their gunpowder weapons were less effective and sought the advice of European experts. They did this more so in the seventeenth than eighteenth centuries, in part because Ming and then Manchu China was more under pressure in the seventeenth.

Second, the 1717 campaign indicates the crucial role of politics in warfare. Chinese success in 1696 owed much to support from Galdan's rebellious nephew, Tsewang Rabtan, and disunity on Lha-bzan's side was important to the result in 1717. His regime rested on force, his army was divided and lacked coherence, and the attack on Lhasa was greatly assisted by traitors within. The major role of politics in conflict is also more generally true. Thus, the Mughal Emperor Aurangzeb's difficult campaign against Maratha-held forts in India in 1699–1704 depended on bribery, a process eased by the nature of loyalty in that society. Torna fell to a surprise night storming in 1704, but in most of the other forts the commanders were bribed to surrender. Similarly, financial–political considerations played a crucial role in the British defeat of the Nawab of Bengal at Plassey in 1757: the Nawab's leading general, Mir Jaffir, had reached an understanding with Robert Clive.

Third, the 1717 Dsungar campaign revealed the importance of cavalry, as did the overrunning of Turkestan in central Asia by the Dsungars in 1724–5. The tactical aspects of cavalry warfare had profound effects on the strategic understanding of what constituted victory. In particular, warfare in the steppes, where there were few strongholds, relied upon very relative degrees of victory. Conditions were extremely fluid and the enemy could always ride away. As a result, leaders had to think about how best to control the situation; gaining some kind of hold over a population without the regular application of force was far from easy. Subsidies and genocide were two possibilities, both (but especially the former) employed at times in Chinese relations with their neighbours. The Manchu used Lamaist Buddhism to control the Mongols and therefore needed to dominate the Tibetan centres of Buddhism. Conflict over Tibet revealed the interaction of steppe and Chinese understandings of victory. It was necessary to determine which was most important: holding territory or defeating the army in the field, the two poles of the Chinese–steppe continuum of warfare.

Cavalry was crucial to the struggle between China and the Dsungars. Such an important role for cavalry is not the

Malay Kris weaponry. Hand-to-hand weapons were more important in the eighteenth century than is often appreciated. These weapons were employed by dynamic powers and people, such as the Nepalese Gurkhas who used swords (kukris). In south-east Asia, war elephants, pikes, swords and spears were still important, and firearms made scant impact on tactics.

impression that emerges from warfare in western Europe or from European operations elsewhere in the world. In these, especially in the latter, infantry predominated, and war centred on the recruitment, deployment and tactical capability of the infantry. Cavalry was of particularly limited value in amphibious operations, such as the Spanish invasion of Sardinia, given the difficulties of transporting and landing horses safely.

It was not only in European operations that infantry predominated; it was also crucial in areas outside the European military tradition, for example the forested regions of coastal west Africa, Amazonia, Ceylon (Sri Lanka), the Himalayas and south-east Asia. But cavalry still dominated warfare in many areas, such as central and south-west Asia, India – apart from Kerala in the south and the waterlogged Ganges plain – and the savannah belt of Africa. Cavalry was also important in eastern Europe: Polish and Russian armies had large numbers of cavalry for fighting on open plains, especially against Turks. However, much of their cavalry was irregular – for example, Cossack forces – and the role of cavalry in European regular armies was less important than it was, for example, in Mughal India.

Far from cavalry becoming less important throughout the world, as was indeed the case in western Europe, it became more so in some regions. This was

OPPOSITE: *Tibetan culture. The expansion of major powers was achieved in part at the expense of long-established cultures such as that of Tibet. Control over Tibetan Buddhism was seen as important to consolidate the Chinese position in Mongolia and to improve Chinese strength in the struggle with the Dsungars.*

Depiction of combat in a Nepalese legend. The Gurkhas were one of the more dynamic south Asian powers. They proved effective in Himalayan conflict and in their tactics made extensive use of ambushes and temporary fortifications, particularly stockades.

Japanese steel arrow heads. Japan was not expansionist in this period, and it was not threatened by China. Its abandonment of gunpowder weaponry in the seventeenth century could therefore be maintained. Increased European naval penetration of the northern Pacific threatened this situation.

certainly the case with the wide expanses of the Great Plains of North America, where the use of the horse spread from Spanish-ruled Mexico northwards, reaching the Cheyenne and Pawnee by 1755, and the Sioux, on the modern Canadian border, by 1770. Both there and in south Asia the horse proved reconciliable with the use of missile weapons, not only the bow and arrow, but also pistols and muskets. Indeed, far from cavalry proving anachronistic, it was to be armies relying on the combination of horse and gun that conquered Persia in 1721–2, and successfully invaded northern India in 1738–9 and 1752–61. However, these campaigns in India, especially the 1738–9 invasion, were actually massive raids; widespread occupation did not follow, in part because infantry would have been needed in order to gain and garrison fortified positions.

In much of Africa the use of cavalry was restricted by the tsetse fly, in south-east Asia by the effects of topography and dense tree cover. Thus, environment was an important constraint on the effectiveness of particular weapons systems, limiting the global impact of technological developments, and affecting the development of particular types of warfare in different regions. For example, the Ganges plain below Patna was very rich but, with its numerous waterways and waterlogged fields, it was bad cavalry country and was usually avoided by cavalry forces.

However, a typology of warfare based on adaptation to environmental factors is limited, not only because no one-dimensional typology is adequate, but also because other important factors may be omitted from such an analysis. One factor that is often forgotten, for example, is the political context; like the environment, this affects what is possible in warfare and thus provides the parameters for the more commonly discussed factors, such as strategy, tactics, weaponry, logistics, leadership and morale.

It is possible to contrast areas of the world with limited state development, such as Patagonia, Amazonia, North America, Australasia, the Pacific and parts of south-west Africa, with others where government was more developed and society more differentiated, such as Japan, China, Burma, Siam, Kandy (the interior of Sri Lanka), India, Persia, the Ottoman empire and much of west Africa. In the former

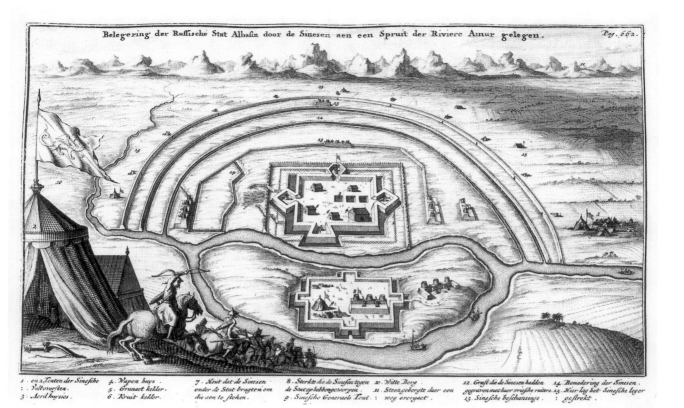

Belegering der Ruſſiſche Stat Albaſin door de Sineſen aen een Spruit der Riviere Amur gelegen.   *Pag. 662.*

1 . en 2 Tenten der Sineſche   4 . Wapen huys .   7 . Hout dat de Sineſen   8 . Sterkte die de Sineſen tegen   10 . Witte Berg .   12 . Gruft die de Sineſen hadden   14 . Benadering der Sineſen .
: . Veltoverſten .   5 . Granaet kelder .   onder de Stat bragten om   de Stat op hebben geworpen .   11 . Steengebergte daer een   gegraven met haer vrieſche ruiters. 15 . Hier lag het Sineſche leger
3 . Aerd huyſies .   6 . Kruit kelder .   die aen te ſteken .   9 . Sineſche Generaels Tent .:   weg overgaet .   13 . Sineſche beſchanſinge .   : geſtrekt .

there was no specialization of the military, and fit adult males were all expected to act as warriors. As the economies of these regions were also limited, mostly dependent on pastoral or shifting cultivation, they supported only relatively small populations, primitive governmental systems and a resource base that could carry neither a large army nor what would later be termed a military–industrial complex. Thus, when in 1763–4 a number of North American tribes fought the British in Pontiac's War, they could not sustain the conflict because they lacked the resources to support long-term campaigning and to replenish their supplies of gunpowder.

More developed societies had evolved more specialization; they had permanent armies and could field and maintain larger forces. They were also able to support wars of expansion, although not all did so. Japan, for instance, did not engage in war at all during this period.

The most dynamic state and the most successful military power in the world, on land, was China. It continued the process of expansion begun in the second half of the seventeenth century when Formosa (Taiwan) was occupied (1683), the Russians were driven from the Amur Valley (1682–9) and the Dsungars were defeated (1696–7). Between 1700 and 1760, China finished off the Dsungars, imposing control as far as Lake Balkhash. It also annexed eastern Turkestan from the Afaqi Makhdumzadas; Kashgar fell in 1759. Expeditions sent against Burma in 1766–9 were less successful, but in 1792 the Chinese advanced to Katmandu, where the Gurkhas of Nepal, whose expansion had begun to

China and Russia clashed in the Amur valley in the 1680s. The Russian fortress of Albazin was successfully besieged in 1685 and 1686 and in 1689 the Chinese advanced as far as Nerchinsk. By the Treaty of Nerchinsk, the Russians acknowledged Chinese control of the valley. The European device of the 'artillery fortress' had proved unable to maintain the European presence.

challenge the Chinese position in Tibet, were forced to recognize Chinese authority. During this period, the Chinese also suppressed a number of major rebellions. By the end of the century China was at peace with all its neighbours, and on China's terms. Russia accepted China's treaty boundaries, but not those of Turkey or Persia; the eastern Mongols were part of the Chinese system; the Dsungars had been destroyed and other neighbours were tributary powers. The next powerful central Asian people to the west, the Kazakhs, accepted tributary status and remained under Chinese influence until it was supplanted by that of Russia in the mid nineteenth century. China's advance was the most astonishing extension of power on land in the eighteenth century. Many Chinese maps of the period show that the empire's extent was unprecedented.

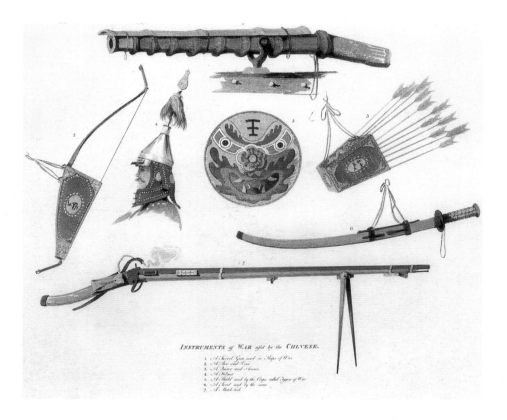

INSTRUMENTS of WAR used by the CHINESE.

1. A Swivel Gun used in Ships of War
2. A Bow and Case
3. A Quiver and Arrows
4. A Helmet
5. A Shield used by the Corps called Tygers of War
6. A Sword used by the same
7. A Match-lock

Chinese weapons, 1794. Chinese forces had less standardized equipment than their European counterparts, but this was not surprising given the size and diversity of Chinese forces and the variety of environments in which they had to fight. They lacked comparable naval forces.

In the Chinese novel *Nü-hsien wai-shih* by Lü Hsiung, published in 1711, the Moon Queen condemned the impact of cannon:

At midnight, Moon Queen, together with Instructress Pao and Instructress Man, went and had a look at the situation of Pei-P'ing so she might point out a strategy. She saw that cannon without number had been placed on top of all the city-walls: Red-Barbarians' cannon, shrapnel-cannon, Heaven-exploding cannon and Divine Mechanism cannon ... Moon Queen said ... 'Such things are not meant for use against people! They turn all who dare to be soldiers into a pulp of flesh. There is no use anymore for the six tactics and three strategies.'

Chinese military post, 1796. Chinese fortifications were less concerned with repelling cannon fire than their European counterparts. China was not threatened at this point on her land or sea frontiers by any power with significant offensive capability. Chinese earth forts were to be surprisingly effective against British warships.

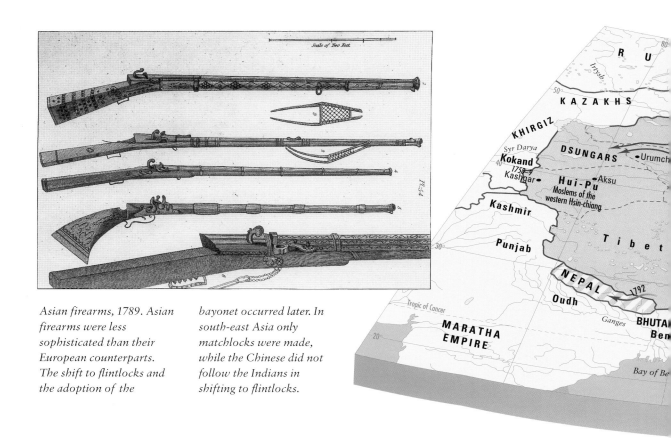

Asian firearms, 1789. Asian firearms were less sophisticated than their European counterparts. The shift to flintlocks and the adoption of the *bayonet occurred later. In south-east Asia only matchlocks were made, while the Chinese did not follow the Indians in shifting to flintlocks.*

Moon Queen then used an amulet to make the cannon ineffective. In fact, although operating more traditionally than the Europeans, the Chinese did not give up the gun, as did the Japanese in the seventeenth century. Firearms had played a major role in Ming warfare. Furthermore, the Manchu conquest of Ming China in the mid seventeenth century had infused the Chinese military with a new dynamic and a greater ability to operate successfully in the steppe, although it did not lead to a military system similar to that of Europe. Cavalry played a larger role in what was in effect a Manchu–Chinese hybrid. The earlier Ming had lacked adequate cavalry, because there was a shortage of adequate cavalry horses in China and they were unable to obtain them in sufficient numbers from the steppe.

The chief characteristic of the Chinese military was a certain remorseless persistence. China had the largest army in the world, but lacked long-range naval capability. This army was impressive in its operational range, acting in very different terrains: in the Gobi Desert and on the Tibetan plateau, for example. Such operations posed problems for both fighting and logistics. Long-range operations were the principal military challenge for China in the eighteenth century: there was no comparable power on China's borders deploying similar forces and the Chinese made no attempt to conquer Japan.

Having clashed in the 1680s, China and Russia avoided fresh hostilities,

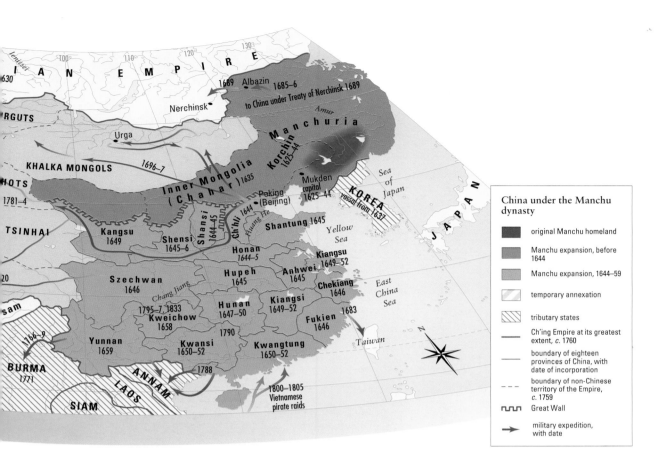

CHINA UNDER THE
MANCHU DYNASTY

*Manchu dynamism throws
into question any analysis of
the period that centres on
European power and
expansion. Manchu China
was the most populous state
in the world and the
strongest land power.*

neither power seeking to revise the frontier agreement reached at Nerchinsk in 1689. Indeed, this agreement was confirmed in the Treaty of Kiakhta in 1728. These treaties stabilized the Chinese frontier and deprived the Dsungars of the possibility of Russian support; despite the distance from the centres of Russian power, this might have been valuable to the Dsungars, not least by providing them with modern cannon. Johan Renat, a Swedish artillery officer in Dsungar service in 1716–33, was employed in making guns and mortars and in teaching the smelting of iron and the manufacture of bullets. In 1733 the Dsungar leader Galdan Tsering showed great interest in Russian weaponry when he met the Russian envoy, but none was provided.

The Dsungars also lacked the support of the Kazakhs, because of earlier attacks upon them: Dsungar cavalry had advanced into central Kazakhstan in 1723. Furthermore, as a result of skilful Chinese diplomacy, owing much to Manchu practices, most of the Mongol princes also refused to help the Dsungars. Thus, the struggle between China and the Dsungars, arguably the most important war on land of the century, far from being a simple clash between settled and nomadic peoples, was the outcome of a much more complex situation.

The crucial factors in Chinese military capability were not weaponry but, rather, the political context and the ability to deliver power at a great distance: in

Burma, Nepal, Tibet and Xinjiang. This matched the situation within the European world: organizational developments, range and capability were more important than military technology in terms of absolute and relative power. In 1720, for example, after advances in each of the two previous years into Tibet, the Chinese army from Szechwan occupied Lhasa. Another Chinese army, advancing from the north-east, repulsed three Dsungar night attacks and reached Lhasa a month later, bringing the campaign to a successful conclusion. Their strategy was based on co-ordinated advances, the same strategy that had been employed against the Dsungars in Mongolia in the 1690s and would be again in Xinjiang in the 1750s. The 1720 advance revealed the characteristic features of Chinese operations: overwhelming force, thorough planning and the ability to act over the long term and at long distance.

These qualities, combined with divisions and smallpox among the Dsungars, again gave victory to the Chinese in the 1750s. The Dsungar ruler, Dawaci, was defeated and captured at the Ili river in 1755, but his rival, Amursana, who had helped the Chinese, then rebelled, leading to another successful Chinese campaign in 1755–7. China under the Manchus successfully solved the logistical problems which no previous dynasty had been able to surmount and discovered how to manage steppe warfare, which was considered the supreme strategic threat by all Chinese dynasties. In the 1750s the Chinese established two chains of magazine posts along the main roads on which they advanced against Dsungaria. Supplies were transported for thousands of miles, and the Mongolian horselands controlled by the Manchus' eastern Mongol allies provided the horses and their fodder. These improvements in logistics – partly due to a desire to keep the troops from alienating the populace – meant that the Chinese armies did not disintegrate as Napoleon's did in Russia in 1812. Just as in Europe where the extension of arable farming in the Ukraine and Hungary served as a base for successful Russian and Austrian operations against the Turks, so the Chinese benefited from the extension of arable farming in Kansu. Furthermore, in order to wage the war there was a massive transfer of resources from eastern to western China – the application to military purposes of the great demographic and agricultural expansion of China of the eighteenth century.

The Chinese were less successful against Burma. War began in 1765 over what had hitherto been the buffer zone of the Shan states. In 1766 the scope of operations widened to include a Chinese invasion of Burma proper. This, and the two subsequent expeditions, were, however, outmanoeuvred by two skilful Burmese generals, Maha Si-thu and Maha Thi-ha Thu-ra, and in 1769 the invading Chinese army was trapped by the latter at Kaung-ton and forced to accept peace. (The British were to face similar limits to imperial power when advancing armies were surrounded and forced to terms – at Saratoga in the Hudson valley of North America in 1777 and at Wadgaon in west India two years later. They were also forced to terms in 1769 by Haidar Ali of Mysore.)

This Chinese failure, repeated against Tongking in northern Vietnam in

1788–9, is a reminder of the dangers of adopting any notion of a scale of military achievement or of advancing a Eurocentric interpretation of military history. The Chinese were less successful along their southern frontiers than they were in central Asia because the area was not of central strategic interest to China (often the generals sent were less competent) and because the heavily forested environment was very difficult for large-scale military operations. In addition, Burmese military organization and achievement had been improved mid century by Alaung-hpaya. This was part of his regeneration of a divided country, and indicates that the causes of military revival and new-found success outside Europe rested primarily not, as is often assumed, on the adoption or adaptation of western technology and/or organization, but rather on indigenous causes. Successful leadership was crucial, as was also to be demonstrated by China under the Kangxi emperor (1662–1723), by Persia under Nadir Shah in the 1730s and 1740s, and, on a lesser scale, by such south Asian rulers as Rudra Singh, the ruler of the Ahom in the Brahmaputra valley of India in 1696–1714, and Gharib Newaz, who revitalized the Manipur state (in modern north-eastern India) in the 1720s and 1730s.

The personal determination of the Kangxi (1662–1723) and Qianlong (1736–98) emperors was crucial to the defeat of the Dsungars. Both made it a personal crusade and pushed hard those generals who were more hesitant about campaigning on the steppes. Kangxi wanted victory, and he understood the transient nature of the possession of territory. The Qianlong emperor wanted to surpass the achievement of his grandfather by putting an end to the frontier problem. The importance of personality is illustrated by the role of the Yongzheng emperor (1723–36), who launched only one expedition against the Dsungars, and did not persist after its failure. Had he ruled as long as his predecessor or successor, the Dsungars might have expanded once again and become a powerful central Asian empire. The reign of Yongzheng was not characterized by major initiatives elsewhere either.

The personalities of generals were also crucial, since the political goal of a campaign dictated not only the means required to pursue it, but also who was employed to lead it and how much power they were given. The ability of rulers who were not personally in command to select appropriate generals was therefore important to success. In the case of China, and many other states, ethnic or racial politics were also important, in terms of the choice of which troops to use and in what combination. The Chinese sought to produce an effective combination of Manchu cavalry and Green Standards troops (Chinese infantry).

Alaung-hpaya's Burmese army followed an organizational pattern that was common to most states: a permanent professional force under the central government was supplemented during a war by conscript levies. However, Burmese warfare was different from that in Europe. First, as with the Turkish janissaries, the permanent force was hereditary in membership. In Burma, it was also hereditary in leadership and was supported by the provision of state land.

Nothing

Soldiers were obliged to grow their own food, a crucial restraint on their operational independence. Second, the weaponry and tactics were also very different from those in Europe. As in Nepal, Sri Lanka and Kerala, tactics involved extensive use of ambushes, ruses and temporary fortifications, especially stockades. Most fighting was with sword and spear, although firearms also played an important role.

Burmese successes indicated that it was not necessary to use Western-style arms in order to prevail. In 1757–8, Alaung-hpaya successfully invaded Manipur and, in 1759, Tenasserim to the south. Although disease and the strength of its fortifications thwarted the Burmese siege of the Siamese capital, Ayuthia, in 1760, a pincer campaign against the city was launched four years later. This led first to the occupation of the lands to the north and south, especially Chiang Mai

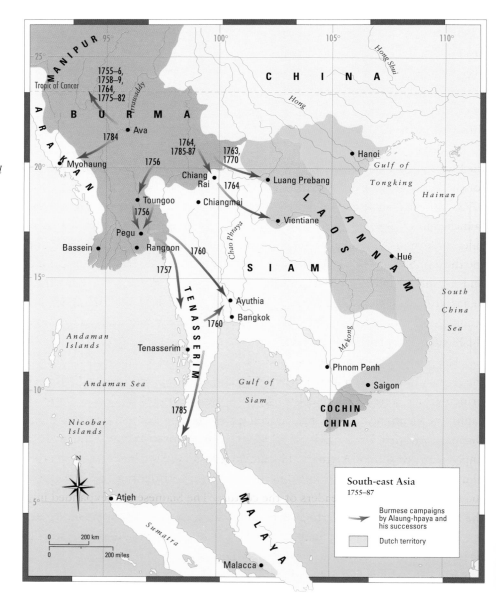

and Laos, although the Burmese force in southern Siam was defeated by P'Ya Tashin at the battle of P'etchaburi in 1764. Nevertheless, the war continued and in 1767 Burmese advances led to the storming of Ayuthia and the capture of the Siamese king. The campaign had persisted through two rainy seasons, the soldiers growing their own rice so that the army did not fade away. In 1784 the independent state of Arakan was overrun and its king and 20,000 of its people were taken to Burma.

These campaigns show the dynamism of the south Asian states. Burma's rulers controlled resources sufficient to deploy large forces: the army of 55,000 men which invaded Manipur in 1765 was larger than the field armies of the English East India Army at this stage. About 200,000 men were conscripted for the 1785 and 1786 expeditions against Siam.

Burmese success was to be challenged by a Siamese revival, first by Tashin and then by Chakri, a general who seized the throne in 1782, becoming Rama I. Tashin raised a new army in northern Siam and recaptured the central area around Ayuthia, but he was unsuccessful when he attacked Chiang Mai. Tashin also defeated two other claimants to the Siamese throne and re-established government control in the country. Between 1770 and 1773 he turned east and, after some difficulty, installed a client ruler in Cambodia. In 1775 Tashin finally drove the Burmese from Chiang Mai.

By driving the Burmese out of Siam and the Lao principalities, Tashin ended the Burmese encirclement of 1764–7 and produced fresh manpower and resources for the Siamese army. A Burmese attempt to repeat the encirclement strategy in 1773 collapsed in the face of rebellions, but fresh Burmese invasions were launched in 1775–6, 1785 and 1786. These were thwarted, the first by a change of ruler in Burma, the second by Siamese attacks on Burmese communications and the third in battle. The 1785 offensive entailed advances on Siam from the north and a pincer offensive on southern Siam. One force moved over land from Tenasserim through the Kra Isthmus towards Junk Ceylon/Phuket Island, while a second force proceeded to the island by sea from Tavoy in Tenasserim. However, the Burmese occupation of Junk Ceylon was very brief.

The struggle between the two powers was one of the most bitter conflicts of the century and greatly affected the neighbouring Lao principalities. In 1776 these principalities were evacuated by the Burmese and in 1778 Tashin invaded, capturing Vientiane and forcing the region to recognize Siamese suzerainty. The Burmese invaded Laos again in 1785. Tashin meanwhile had launched an unpopular invasion of Vietnam. His growing insanity led Chakri to overthrow him in 1782 and Tashin was killed in the resulting street fighting. He was one of the most impressive war leaders of the century. The Siamese also expanded into the Malay peninsula, reasserting suzerainty over the northern Malay sultanates.

Burmese failure against Siam reflected leadership factors on the two sides, the development of effective defensive strategies by the Siamese and the role of geopolitical and internal political factors. The rise of commitments on Burma's

OPPOSITE: *Bodyguard of Ranjit Singh, founder of Sikh state, on horseback with matchlock guns. Singh united the Sikh clans and in 1799 established Sikh dominance in the Punjab. His success was a product of Mughal weakness.*

Son of Shah Hüseyin, Shah Tahmasp II contested the seizure of Persia by the Ghilzai Afghans and called on the Turks for aid. Persia's continuity in the crises of the 1720s and 1730s indicated the resilience of governmental units. Persia was not digested by aggressive neighbours as Poland was in 1772–95.

western frontier, as in Arakan, was important, and a reminder of the need to consider a state's military effectiveness and strategic choices by looking at the totality of its commitments.

Examples of the latter can also be found in south-west Asia. The Ottoman Turks are usually considered solely as an opponent of Christian powers, but it is necessary to remember the Turkish conflict with Persia, which became important from the 1720s after over eighty years of peace. Indeed, Persia provides an example of the crucial role of leadership in military activity and in the possibility of military revival in this period. The Safavid empire had been overthrown from the east by the Ghilzai Afghans in 1721–2. This was a triumph, both strategic and tactical, over the poor leadership of Shah Hüseyin (1694–1724). The Afghans used fire-power, and in 1722 they employed sixty *zanbūrak* – camel-mounted swivel guns – at the battle of Gulnabad, in which the Persians were defeated.

However, political stability eluded the Ghilzai leader, Mahmud. Hüseyin's son, Tahmasp, declared himself Shah Tahmasp II in Tabriz and turned to the neighbouring Turks, the traditional enemy, for aid. They overran western Persia. Mahmud, meanwhile, was murdered in 1725 and the succession was contested by his son and a nephew, who were driven from Persia by Nadir Kuli, a Turcoman

tribesman, in 1729–30. Nadir Shah put Tahmasp on the Persian throne and defeated the Turks at Nahavand, near Hamadan, in 1730; this was one of the decisive battles of the century, for it ensured that western Persia would remain outside the Turkish orbit.

Out of the ensuing chaos Nadir emerged, first as strong man and then as ruler. He campaigned in every direction, fighting not only a long war against the Turks, defeating Topal Osman Pasa near Kirkuk in 1733 and Abdullah Köprülü at Baghavand in 1735, but also advancing into Daghestan in the Caucasus, and Afghanistan, Oman and India. Indeed, his other commitments prevented Nadir Shah from exploiting victories over the Turks in 1730 and 1733 and invading their

Persia in the eighteenth century 1719–45

- Persian advances
- attacks by Mahmud and the Ghaznis
- Turkish attacks
- Russian attacks
- ✕ battle, with date
- Persia
- area disputed with Ottomans 1512–1639
- territories taken from Mughal Empire
- Ottoman Empire 1550
- Russia 1730
- occupied by Russia 1722–32
- other states and territories

Anatolian heartland, although in Constantinople it was feared that he would. On both occasions he had to deal with opposition to the east, in 1730 in Afghanistan and in 1733 a revolt in Baluchistan.

In 1736, after the death of Tahmasp's son, Nadir became shah. His subsequent invasion of India was the most spectacular episode of his career. Having conquered southern Afghanistan in 1736 and Kabul and Kandahar in 1738, Nadir Shah invaded northern India the following year, capturing Peshawar and Lahore, and defeating the Mughal Emperor, Muhammad II, at Karnal, north of Delhi. He then sacked the city, which had fallen without resistance. As a result, the Mughals ceded Sind and all territories west of the Indus to Nadir Shah. This

was a victory for the determined leadership of mobile forces. Nadir Shah used mounted musketeers, but it was their mobility, rather than their fire-power, which was crucial, although his camel-mounted swivel guns made an impact on the Indian cavalry.

Having returned from India, Nadir Shah conquered the khanates of Bukhara and Khiva in central Asia (1740) and he then campaigned unsuccessfully in Daghestan (1741–3), before resuming war with the Turks (1742–6). He was repelled from Mosul and Baghdad (the major Turkish bases in modern Iraq) but he captured Kirkuk (1743), defeated the Turks at Kars (1745) and overran Armenia. The Turks found it difficult to operate successfully so far from their centre of military power, Constantinople (modern Istanbul). Nadir Shah's military power was also typical of south and east Asian states in its emphasis on land, not sea, forces. He developed a fleet in the 1730s in order to intervene in Oman, but did not persist with it after 1744. This neglect only increased under his successors.

Nadir Shah was the Napoleon of south Asia, a usurper who rose from humble beginnings to occupy the throne of Persia and seize the Peacock Throne of the Mughals as booty. On a small-scale map of the world his achievements may not seem so great, but he campaigned over a vast area, from Delhi to Baghdad, Khiva to Muscat, Daghestan to Kashmir. He expanded the Persian state more than did any of the Safavids who had ruled it from the beginning of the sixteenth century.

PERSIA IN THE EIGHTEENTH CENTURY

Safavid Persia had not been a dynamic power in the late seventeenth century but, once taken over by Nadir Shah, Persia fulfilled its geopolitical potential as a state able to act in South Asia, the Caucasus, the Middle East and the Persian Gulf.

Third battle of Panipat, 14 January 1761. The scale of the engagement and the numbers of combatants and casualties should have ensured that this would be as well known as the major battles of the Seven Years War. Panipat indicated the continued importance of cavalry, the role of reserves, and the importance of responsive generalship. The Afghan leader, Ahmad Khan, proved tactically the equal of Marlborough.

Nadir Shah was not always successful, but he won a series of major battles. Like Napoleon, he was a bold practitioner of warfare; he put the emphasis on mobility and made the areas he campaigned in support his forces. A bold ruler, who, like Peter the Great of Russia and Rama I of Siam, moved the capital city, in his case eastward from Isfahan to Meshed (in theirs, Moscow to St Petersburg and Ayuthia to Bangkok), Nadir sought to resolve the schism within Islam, and to integrate Shi'ism into Sunn'ism. Like Napoleon, his continual wars and heavy taxation placed a considerable burden on his subjects and led to revolts. And, again like Napoleon, his empire proved ephemeral. It split apart after he was assassinated in 1747.

Although battles played the major role in warfare in south-west Asia, sieges could also be important. Thus, the Safavid monarchy collapsed when Isfahan surrendered in October 1722 due to food shortages caused by a seven-month siege. The Afghans had successfully besieged the Persian fortress of Kirman the previous year, and it too fell to blockade: starvation worked where direct assaults had failed. Kandahar, with its mud walls, was taken by Nadir Shah in 1738 after a nine-month siege. Like other rulers in the region, he preferred battles to sieges because sieges posed a logistical challenge and it could be difficult to maintain the cohesion and morale of a besieging army composed in large part of tribal levies. Partly for this reason, a series of fortified cities – Kars, Mosul, Kirkuk, Baghdad, Tabriz, Hamadan and Kirmanshah – played a major role in the course of the Persian–Turkish hostilities. Similarly, fortresses could be important in struggles between Islamic powers further west: in 1787 and 1793, Kara Mahmoud, the rebellious governor of Scutari (in modern Albania) was able to retreat into the citadel and hold it, for three months each time, against the forces of the Turkish Sultan, before defeating the besiegers in an attack concerted with allies from outside the fortress.

The invasion of India in 1739 was not the last to be launched from Afghanistan. After Nadir Shah was assassinated, the eastern part of his empire passed into the hands of Ahmad Khan (1747–73), the founder of the Durrani empire. He repeatedly attacked north-west India in the 1750s, annexing Lahore, Kashmir and Multan in 1752 and Sirhind in 1757. These attacks culminated in his victory over the Maratha confederation, then the leading power in India, at the third battle of Panipat, north of Delhi, on 14 January 1761, probably the largest land battle of the century. This battle reflected the continued role of cavalry and helps to explain why the military challenge that many Indian rulers were seeking to resist was not that of British infantry. The Afghan forces under Ahmad Khan consisted largely of heavy cavalry equipped with body armour and muskets. Their Maratha opponents, roughly equal in numbers, included the traditional mobile light cavalry, armed with swords, shields, battleaxes, daggers and lances, and the trained infantry of one commander, Ibrahim Gardi. The Marathas had little experience in integrating the different military capabilities of their various units, in particular the need to combine the offensive characteristics of their light cavalry with the more stationary tactics required by the artillery and infantry, who needed the cavalry to defend their flanks from opposing cavalry.

The Marathas, blockaded in a fortified position at Panipat by the Afghans, had lost their mobility. When they came out of their positions, their faces were anointed with saffron, a sign that they had come out to conquer or die. The battle began at dawn after a fierce discharge of artillery and rockets in which the Maratha gunners, probably deceived by the light, fired high. Nevertheless, the Marathas pushed back the Afghans, who were initially only able to hold their own on their left flank. But while the Maratha infantry advanced in disciplined order, driving back the opposing Ruhela matchlock men, there was no co-ordination with their undisciplined cavalry. The Maratha cavalry advances were checked, and the slow-moving cannon failed to keep up. In short, the absence of a satisfactory command structure exacerbated problems of control caused by the composite nature of the Maratha army.

While the Ruhelas on the Maratha right were hard pressed, in the centre the Maratha advance drove back their opponents. In the late afternoon, however, Ahmad committed his 5,000-strong cavalry reserves and Afghan attacks were launched simultaneously all along the line. The Marathas lacked reserves and were exhausted; their men and horses had had little food for weeks, and none since dawn. Nevertheless, they fought hard until resistance collapsed at about four o'clock. Nearly all Ibrahim's unit died fighting. In the face of the Afghan cavalry attacks the Maratha centre disintegrated and there was a general rout, with the death of many of the Maratha commanders. The Afghans pursued the fleeing Marathas all night, killing many. The following morning, the camp was stormed and many more Marathas were killed. The prisoners were all beheaded.

Panipat was only the most spectacular of the Indian battles, Ahmad Khan only one of the new dynasts who rose from the ruins of the Mughal empire; the decline of the leading Indian dynasty in the last years of Aurangzeb's reign and even more after his death in 1707, provided provincial potentates with the opportunity and also the need to grasp power. Thus Asaf Jah, the Nizam of Hyderabad, defeated the governor of Khandesh at Shakarkhera in 1724 and became in effect independent, sundering what had been one of the major achievements of the Mughals, the control of Hindustan (northern India) over the Deccan (central south India). The Nawab of Bengal in east India also became independent in 1733.

This process interacted with the continued challenge of the Marathas of west India and their raiding light cavalry. They pressed hard on the Nizam, defeating him at battles such as Bhopal (1738), Bhalke (1752) and Udgir (1760). In 1740 some 50,000 Marathas invaded the Carnatic in south-east India, defeating and killing the Nawab of the Carnatic at the battle of Damalcherry and then pressing on to capture Arcot (1740) and Trichinopoly (1741). The Jats were defeated at Bharatpur in 1770. The Marathas were not the sole aggressive force in India, however. One opposing general, Haidar Ali, seized power in Mysore in 1761 and then began a process of expansion in southern India, although he was defeated by the Marathas at Chinkurali in 1771. Further north, successive conquests spread Gurkha power along the Himalayan chain.

Although the Gurkhas in their mountainous terrain relied on infantry, both the Marathas and Haidar Ali concentrated on light cavalry. The Marathas were more mobile than the slow-moving Mughal armies and concentrated on cutting them off from supplies and reinforcements. The Mughals were routed at Talkatora in 1738. Similar tactics were successful for the Marathas, both against the Nizam and in attacks on Bengal, but, from mid century, the Marathas felt it increasingly necessary to supplement their cavalry with infantry and artillery in order to be more effective against fortresses and to take advantage of developments in muskets. The added cost of these disrupted the political economy of Maratha warfare and increased the cost of armed forces. Mysore also supplemented their cavalry with artillery; when the British took Bangalore from Mysore forces in 1791, they found over 100 cannon. Further west, however, cavalry remained the crucial arm of the Persians. In 1795 Georgia, abandoned by its Russian ally, was overrun by Agha Muhammad's Persian cavalry, and the capital Tbilisi was sacked, with heavy casualties.

The feudal cavalry of the Turks, the *sipahis*, was less important in battle than the janissary infantry, by now a hereditary caste. The *sipahis* had once been a dynamic force, but increasingly acted as a repository of conservative military practice. An inability to pay the army regularly reduced governmental control, and led to rebellions, for example in 1687, 1717, 1718, 1719 and 1730.

There were impulses of military reform in the Ottoman (Turkish) empire, generally linked to a desire to emulate the West and often organized by renegade Westerners. Ibrahim Müteferrika, a Hungarian renegade who founded a Turkish printing press, argued, in his publications of the 1730s, including his *Usul ul-Hikam fi Nizam al-Umam* of 1731, for major changes in military organization, better training and discipline, geometric troop formations, volley fire and improved co-operation between infantry and cavalry, in emulation of the military reforms of Peter the Great in Russia. In the 1730s, a French noble, Comte Claude-Alexandre de Bonneval, sought to develop a modern artillery service and a modern corps of bombardiers, but he was thwarted by janissary and political opposition. A French-trained Hungarian nobleman, Baron François de Tott, again concentrated on the Turkish artillery in the 1770s. In the 1790s, after serious defeats at the hands of Austria and Russia in the years 1787–92, the new sultan, Selim III, sought to reform the *sipahis* and janissaries and developed the Nizam-i Cedid, a new army trained and commanded by Western officers. However, the hostility of the janissaries helped to thwart Selim's plans too.

Aside from waging war against the armies of opposing states – Austria, Persia and Russia – the Turkish forces were also expected to suppress rebellions, especially in Egypt in the 1720s and 1780s, and to maintain authority over the nomadic tribesmen of the Arab borderlands. The Arabs had little defence against

Turkish cannon, and sought to avoid such engagements.

The role of martial peoples, tribes and groups in India, most obviously the Marathas, was replicated elsewhere, for example in the Caucasus, in Persia and in the Ottoman empire. Increasingly, such peoples adopted firearms. For example, the Baluchis (of modern Pakistan) used the bow and arrow in the seventeenth century, but acquired firearms in the early 1700s. The Lezgis in the Caucasus had made a similar shift by the 1720s. In the first half of the century, in the East Indies and the Malay world, the Bugis of south Sulawesi were particularly notable as a martial race. Their dynamism and reputation as fighters, with intimidating chants and war dances, and chainmail armour, ensured that they were useful as mercenaries and feared as adversaries. They operated by sea and by land.

The sizeable forces, heavy casualties and long-lasting struggle that marked Panipat differed greatly from those of warfare in America and Australasia amongst indigenous peoples. In both, numbers were far smaller. As a

Chasse générale du Chevreuil.

T. 2. p. 71.

result, there was more emphasis on the individual prowess of warriors. Furthermore, conflict was in some respects not unlike hunting, both because opponents could be regarded as akin to animals – as, for example, in North America – and because emphasis was on the individual, who was pitted against other individuals and against the environment. Furthermore, men hunted and fought, while women were usually responsible for agriculture.

Although there were no large armies on the south Asian model in Australasia and in the New World, it would be misleading to think that there was no organized conflict. On the contrary, Native Americans had developed effective

Half-moon tactic. This Native American hunting tactic was also used in warfare, and proved effective in advance and retreat. The sophisticated nature of native tactics has been underrated. Native rank and file was disciplined and led by capable officers.

tactical formations, especially the half-moon, and a form of warfare well attuned to the forested nature of much of the eastern half of the continent, with ambushes, ruses and feints, and a combination of accurately aimed fire and an astute use of cover. The latter was more important than the weapon which was used, whether bow and arrow or musket, although musket shot was less likely to be deflected by vegetation. The organization and planning required can be compared with that of the bison drives on the Great Plains of North America. But war required more pre-planning than hunting; some native groups, such as the Foxes, created fortifications, timber palisades and trenches.

Warfare in North America was affected by the spread of muskets and horses. The side which acquired them first dominated; once both sides in a conflict had them, the nature of warfare altered. The arrival of the horse brought a far greater mobility, allowing the Native Americans to follow herds of bison or deer for hundreds of miles, and the resulting improvement in diet led to a larger and healthier population. Tribal warfare was affected by trade and animal movements, and by competition for hunting grounds. Thus, at the beginning

Great Plains buffalo (bison) hunt. The spread of the horse brought mobility, permitting Native Americans to follow herds of bison or deer for hundreds of miles. Buffalo drives required much organization and planning and served as preparation for human conflict.

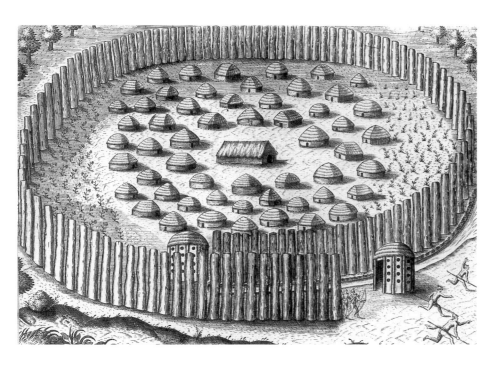

of the century, the Cree fought the Chipewyans, while the Assiniboine were defeated by the Blackfoot. The Cree fought the Dakota Sioux west of Lake Superior, and were still doing so at the end of the century, when a new struggle broke out between the Assiniboine and the Mandan. Raids and ambushes played major roles in conflict, for example that of the Foxes and the Illinois in the 1720s, or, further south-west, the Comanches and the Penxaye Apaches in the 1700s, the Navajos and the southern Utes from the 1710s to the 1750s, and the Utes and the Comanches in the second half of the century. Firearms came to play an important role and the warfare had lasting results; the Comanches, for example, drove the Apaches into the south-west of the modern USA.

Small migratory hunting groups formed the population of much of North America; the same was true to an even greater extent in Australia, and there the absence of horse and gun limited the capacity of humans to kill either each other or animals. Without the horse, distance was a far greater obstacle to

Warriors of New South Wales, 1813. The skeleton pattern of white pigment designed to intimidate opponents had little effect on British troops armed with muskets.

human activity, especially where such activity was organized. Across the Pacific, the situation was varied. In some island groups, such as Hawaii and New Zealand, higher population density and more developed social and political systems enhanced the possibilities of military action. Thus the Napoleon of Hawaii, Kamehameha I, fought his way to supremacy over the archipelago in the 1790s, using muskets and cannon and winning victories such as Nuuanu (1795). The so-called unification of the Hawaiian islands was far from predetermined, however. Kamehameha won dominance of his home island of Hawaii in 1791 and of the islands of Maui and Oahu in 1795. In 1810 Kaumualii, the ruler of the islands of Kauai and Niihau, agreed to serve as a client king to Kamehameha.

This was very different to the level of military attainment across much of the Pacific, or in the Andaman islands in the Indian Ocean, or in Amazonia in South America. A similar variety characterized Africa: areas of low population density and limited governmental development, such as the Kalahari desert of south-west

Kamehameha I of Hawaii fought his way to supremacy in the Hawaiian archipelago in the 1790s in part thanks to his use of European arms, rather than spears, clubs, daggers and sling-shots. His power was based on the west coast of the island of Hawaii, a coast frequented by European ships, and he employed Europeans as gunners.

An entrance to the palace of the Oba of Benin. Muskets replaced javelins and bows as missile weapons in Benin in the early eighteenth century, and missile warfare replaced hand-to-hand fighting. This shift led to an emphasis on volley fire.

Bodyguard of Sheikh of Bornu from Dixon Denham, Narrative of Travels and Discoveries in Northern and Central Africa *(1826). A Peninsular War veteran, he crossed the Sahara in 1822–3, and accompanied Bornu troops on expeditions in 1823.*

Africa, had a different level of military preparedness and warfare from that of polities able to deploy armies of considerable size. In the Horn of Africa in the 1760s, Mikail Sehul, the Ethiopian imperial Ras, built up an army and equipped 8,000 of them with muskets. He defeated his master, Emperor Iyoas in 1769, only to fall victim to the shock tactics of another provincial potentate, Bäwändwässan of Bägémeder, in 1771. By 1790 the Merina of Madagascar could raise an army of 20,000 men.

There was interaction between environment and politics in the processes of

military transformation. In the forest zone of west Africa muskets replaced the bow and javelin in the armies of states, such as Dahomey on the Slave Coast and Asante on the Gold Coast, that were able to obtain arms; this led to more dispersed fighting formations and techniques. The kingdom of Dahomey owed its rise under Agaja (*c.* 1716–40) to an effective use of European firearms combined with standards of training and discipline that impressed European observers; weaponry alone was not enough. However, in the savannah zone, further north, the adoption of muskets by cavalry made relatively little difference to tactics. Clashes between cavalry-centred and infantry-dominated armies occurred along the ecological borderline. Dahomey was subjected to invasions by the cavalry of Oyo in a series of conflicts between 1726 and 1748; although the cavalry could be held off by musketeers sheltering behind field fortifications, their mobility enabled them to pillage Dahomey and force it to surrender and pay tribute. Asante, which sought to expand further west, could not defeat the cavalry of the savannah and became reliant on winning allies who had their own cavalry. Away from the forest belt, the cavalry of the Tuareg conquered Timbuktu on the River Niger in 1787 and, in what is now Sudan west of the White Nile, Kordofan fell to Darfur three years later.

The emphasis on cavalry in the savannah was not the only restriction on the development of infantry–firearms combinations. Whereas in the kingdom of Kongo, in western Angola and on the Slave Coast, musketeers largely replaced archers during the course of the century, as they had done on the Gold Coast the previous century, further away from the Atlantic coast and its European influences there was greater reliance on the traditional system of forest Africa: shield-carrying, heavily armed infantry fighting hand to hand, particularly with swords. In so far as there were missile weapons in support they were generally bows and javelins, not muskets. This was true of such armies as those of Matamba, Kasanje, Muzumbo a Kalunga, and Lunda (in modern eastern Angola). Lunda expansionism is a reminder of the folly of assuming that European-style weaponry and military organization was a precondition for military success.

In Africa, as in most of the non-European world, military capability was largely a matter of land power. However, there were also a series of coastal polities that controlled flotillas operating in inshore, estuarine, deltaic and riverine waters. These boats were shallow in draught and therefore enjoyed a range denied European warships. Their crews usually fought with missile weapons, which in the eighteenth century increasingly meant muskets, and some canoes also carried cannon. In west Africa, coastal settlements based on island lagoons successfully defied Dahomey.

Similar forces existed elsewhere in African waters. The Betsimisaraka and Sakalava of Madagascar developed fleets of outrigger canoes and by the end of the century these could raid as far as the mainland of northern Mozambique. Similar technology was also employed in the Pacific, in New Zealand and in Pacific North America. Again, the divide between the hunting of animals and conflict with humans was not too great at this level of weapon technology and military organization.

By 1789 Kamehameha I of Hawaii was using a swivel gun secured to a platform on the hulls of a big double canoe. Soon after he had a large double canoe mounting two cannon and rigged like a European schooner. Such boats helped him as he expanded his power across the archipelago, but in 1796 and 1809 the difficult waters between Oahu and Kauai, and outbreaks of disease, ended his plans to invade Kauai.

More substantial navies were deployed by only a handful of non-European powers, principally the Ottoman empire, Persia, the Barbary States of north Africa – Morocco, Algiers, Tunis and Tripoli – the Omani Arabs based on Muscat in Arabia and the Maratha Angria family on the Konkan coast of India.

Kanembo spearmen and Munga archers in service of Bornu. An important Islamic state based near Lake Chad, Bornu had reached its greatest extent around 1600, but, thereafter, ceased to be expansionist. Bornu largely dispensed with firearms in the seventeenth century.

The ships of these powers had a greater range than war canoes and approximated more closely to European warships, but they lacked the destructive power of the latter. This was because the Barbary, Omani and Angria ships were commerce raiders where the emphasis was on speed and manoeuvrability, whereas the heavy, slow ships of the line of European navies were designed for battle, where the emphasis was on battering power. However, just as it is inappropriate to neglect non-European armies in any account of eighteenth-century land warfare, so it is misleading to imagine that only the Europeans deployed warships or that their warships were necessarily better. This was especially true of inshore waters and of river fleets, where boats with a shallow draught had the advantage. It was far from clear that European military effectiveness was paramount. However, the principal clashes between European and non-European forces were on land, and it is to these that we must now turn.

Outside Europe, a great variety of weapons was used, particularly non-gunpowder weapons. Their continued effectiveness should not be underrated. LEFT: *Sword and scabbard from Shamshir, Taipan;* RIGHT: *Indian quiver and arrows from Mahratta, Gwalior.*

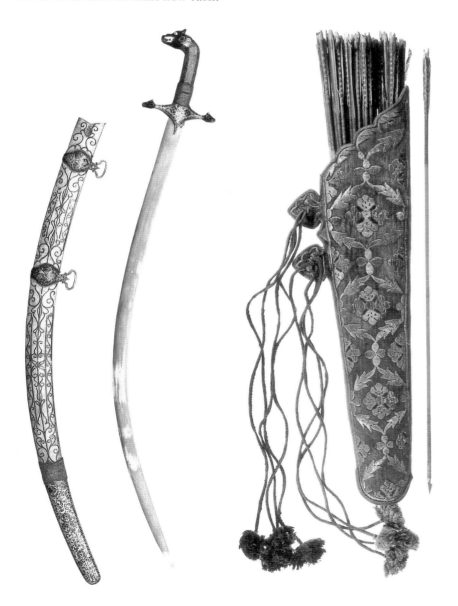

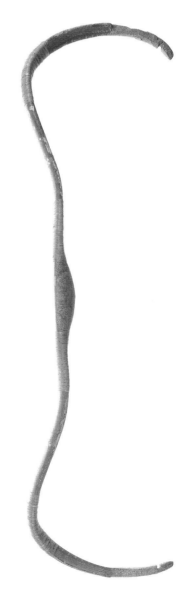

CHAPTER TWO

EUROPEANS VERSUS NON-EUROPEANS

IROQUOIS WARRIOR. *Effective warriors, many of whom chose neutrality in Anglo-French conflicts. They suffered from their dependence on European firearms and, in particular, gunpowder, and from divisions. The Iroquois remained a formidable force into the second half of the century. John Sullivan's campaign against the Iroquois in 1778 was unsuccessful.*

EUROPEANS VERSUS NON-EUROPEANS

A N UNDERSTANDING OF the vitality and viability of non-European forces, as described in the previous chapter, is a precondition for any assessment of their conflicts with European armies. These wars were important in shifting control over important areas of the world, such as much of eastern North America and southern Ukraine, and Bengal in India. The conflicts can be divided into three categories. First, wars along the long frontier between European and Asian states, from the Balkans to Siberia; second, conflicts between long-established European settlement colonies and their neighbours, as in North and South America, and around the Dutch colony of Cape Town, where the Xhosa fought the Dutch Boers towards the close of the century; and third, conflicts where there was no frontier of European settlement, for example in India and Ceylon (Sri Lanka).

Wars between European and Asian countries illustrate the variety of military systems of the period. The Europeans found themselves opposed by the large armed forces of the Ottoman (Turkish) empire and by the small forces of the aboriginal peoples of north-eastern Siberia, the Chukchi, Itelmen and Koryaks, who were armed with bone- or stone-tipped arrows and whose only firearms were those captured from the Russians. In between, both geographically and in terms of the sophistication of weaponry and military organization, came the horsemen of the lands between the Caspian and China, some semi-nomadic, such as the Kazakhs, Kalmyks and the Bashkirs, and some more settled, such as the khanates of central Asia.

Military success did not correspond to this hierarchy. The Russians found the conquest of the frozen fastnesses of Siberia an intractable task: distance, climate, terrain and the determination of their opponents more than made up for the superior Russian fire-power. The Russians could anchor their presence with fortresses, but these could only achieve so much. Although they were difficult for the native peoples to overrun, the fortresses did not really dominate the surrounding countryside and they had to be supplied by vulnerable convoys. This was a war of raids and destruction, of ambushes not battles. Although the Itelmen and Koryaks of Kamchatka were crushed, after genocidal conflicts in

Peter the Great (1672–1725) had a dynamic effect within Russia. With his determined emphasis on novelty and a breach with the past, he marked a potentially radical departure in the use of state power within Europe. In practice, novelty and radicalism were tempered by the weakness of the administration.

1706, 1731, 1741 and 1745–56, the Chukchi of north-east Siberia successfully resisted attacks in 1729–31 and 1744–7, and the Russians were obliged to recognize the Chukchi rights to their territories.

In contrast, in the Balkans and to the north of the Black Sea there was a more direct clash between armies. In neither case was success a foregone conclusion. The Turks won some important campaigns: in 1711 fast-moving Turkish cavalry outmanoeuvred the Russian army under Peter the Great, who had invaded Moldavia (in modern Romania), but found far less local support than he had anticipated. Advancing slowly, the Russians lost the initiative. By advancing as a single force they increased their already serious logistical problems and made it

Map by Jakob Folkema (1692–1767). Exploration was crucial to the expansion of European knowledge, trade and power. European knowledge of the Pacific greatly increased. There were also major gains in information about the interior of North America. No other culture was so active in exploration.

easier for the Turks to encircle them. Surrounded on the banks of the River Pruth, short of food and water, and under fire from the Turkish artillery, Peter was forced to accept humiliating terms.

In 1715 the Venetians were driven from the Morea (the Peloponnese in southern Greece) by the Turks in one of the most decisive campaigns of the century. In 1739 the Austrians were driven back into Belgrade by the Turks and their frightened generals surrendered. The size of the Turkish empire created serious operational problems, but it also enabled the movement of resources in order to focus strength on a particular opponent, so increasing their military effectiveness.

Nevertheless, the balance of advantage rested with Turkey's opponents. Other Turkish advances were successfully resisted, for example by the Venetians in Corfu in 1717 and by Montenegro in 1796. Repeated blows were struck against the Turks by Austria in 1716–18 and 1788–90 and by Russia in 1736–9, 1768–74 and 1787–92. These Turkish defeats were not limited to land, as in the last two the Turkish fleet was defeated by the Russians, most spectacularly at the battle of Cesmé in 1770, when Russian fireships wreaked havoc. On land, the Turks lost battles and saw their fortresses repeatedly fall to siege.

These defeats contrasted with earlier Turkish successes in the sixteenth century, suggesting that there had been a fundamental shift in the balance of

OVERLEAF: *Conflict in the Mediterranean between Venetians and Turks, 1689. Helped by Turkish concentration on war with Austria, Francesco Morosino proved successful in amphibious operations in Greece, although, having taken Athens in 1687, damaging the Parthenon, he had to withdraw in 1688.*

CASPIAN SEA TO THE CHINESE FRONTIER

This vast area witnessed both Chinese and Russian expansion, but also Persian and Afghan advances.

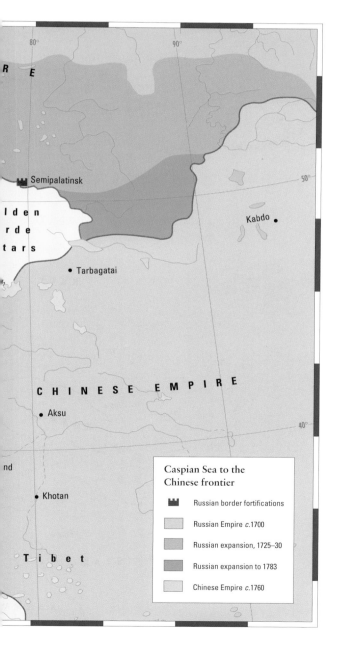

Caspian Sea to the Chinese frontier

- Russian border fortifications
- Russian Empire *c.*1700
- Russian expansion, 1725–30
- Russian expansion to 1783
- Chinese Empire *c.*1760

FRAN:CO MOROSNI: CAPN GNÃLE INSEGVISC
NVMEROSA ASSAI DELLA VENETA, ARRIV
PRENDE.

RMATA TVRCA, CHE FVGGE SEBENE PIV
E DELLE PIV GROSSE GALERE, E LE
E   1659.

THE BALKANS

Although the collapse of the Turkish empire was frequently predicted, the Turks showed great determination and resilience and were particularly successful in checking the Austrian advance.

Battle of Belgrade, 1717. Belgrade was a major focus of the struggle between Austria and the Turks. As at Vienna in 1683, the crucial struggle was between a besieging and a relief army, but in this case the besieging army took the initiative and won.

military advantage, a true military revolution. This began with the Turkish failure to win any essential success in the long war of 1593–1606 with Austria. The Turks were defeated at St Gotthard in 1664 and more severely outside Vienna in 1683. The pace of Turkish defeat then accelerated in the wars that lasted until 1699, settling the fate of Hungary. On 5 August 1716 the Austrians under Prince Eugene smashed the Turks at Peterwardein: the Austrian cavalry drove their opponents from the field, leaving the exposed janissaries to be decimated. As many as 30,000 Turks, including the Grand Vizier, Silahdar Ali Pasha, the Sultan's son-in-law, were killed. Eugene then marched on Temesvár, which had defied the Austrians during the previous war, and which controlled or threatened much of eastern Hungary. Well-fortified and protected by river and marshes, Temesvár nevertheless surrendered on 23 October after heavy bombardment. On 16 August the following year, outside Belgrade, a surprise attack through the fog by Eugene defeated the Turks, leading to the surrender of Belgrade six days later. The battle was a confused engagement, not a matter of neat formations exchanging fire. Although the Austrian victory cannot be simply attributed to the character of European fire-power, the engagement did reveal the battlefield quality of some European units in the face of greater numbers. The Turks made peace in 1718, ceding the rest of Hungary, northern Serbia and western Romania.

In the Russo-Turkish war of 1736–9, the Russians in 1736 stormed the earthworks which barred the isthmus of Perekop at the entrance to the Crimea.

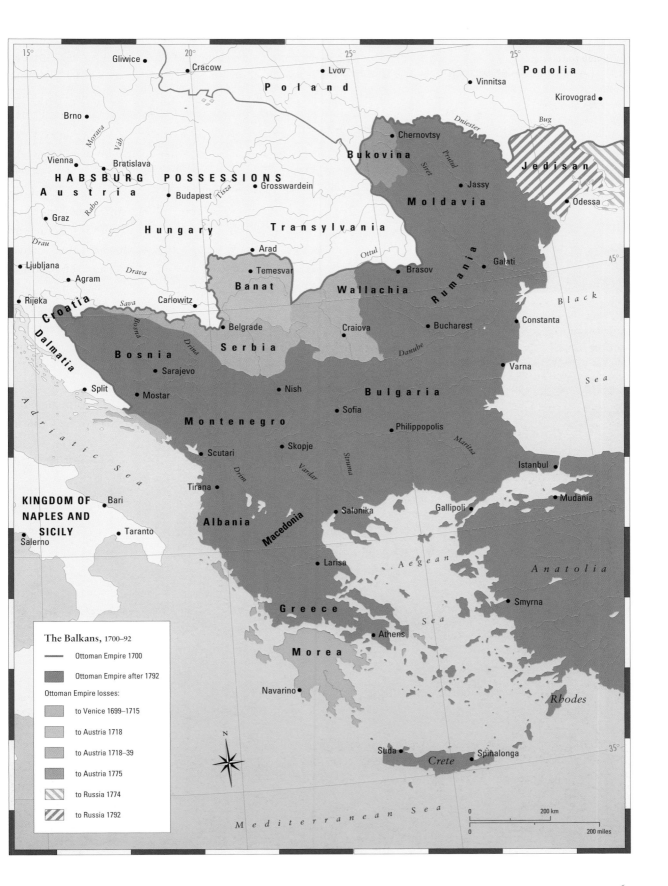

15°
Gliwice •
20°
• Cracow
• Lvov
25°
P o l a n d
25°
P o d o l i a
• Vinnitsa
• Kirovograd

Brno •

Vienna •
• Bratislava
Dniester
Bug
• Chernovtsy
J e d i s a n
B u k o v i n a
Siret
Prutul
• Odessa

H A B S B U R G   P O S S E S S I O N S
• Grosswardein
M o l d a v i a
• Jassy

A u s t r i a

• Graz
Rabo

H u n g a r y
Tisza
T r a n s y l v a n i a
45°

Ljubljana •
Drau
• Budapest
• Arad
Ottul
• Brasov
• Galati
B l a c k

Drava
• Temesvar
R u m a n i a
• Agram

Rijeka •
Sava
Carlowitz
B a n a t
• Belgrade
W a l l a c h i a
• Craiova
• Bucharest
• Constanta
C r o a t i a
Bosna
S e r b i a
S e a

D a l m a t i a
Drina
Danube
• Varna

B o s n i a
• Sarajevo
• Nish
B u l g a r i a

• Split
• Mostar
• Sofia

M o n t e n e g r o
• Philippopolis
Maritsa

A d r i a t i c   S e a
• Scutari
• Skopje
Vardar
Struma
• Istanbul

Tirana •
Drin
• Mudania

KINGDOM OF
• Bari
• Salonika
Gallipoli •
40°

NAPLES AND
A l b a n i a
M a c e d o n i a
A n a t o l i a

SICILY
• Taranto
Salerno •
A e g e a n
• Smyrna

• Larisa

G r e e c e
S e a

• Athens

The Balkans, 1700–92
M o r e a

——— Ottoman Empire 1700
• Navarino
R h o d e s

Ottoman Empire after 1792

Ottoman Empire losses:
35°

to Venice 1699–1715
N
• Suda
• Spinalonga

to Austria 1718
C r e t e

to Austria 1718–39

to Austria 1775

to Russia 1774
0   200 km

to Russia 1792
M e d i t e r r a n e a n   S e a
0   200 miles

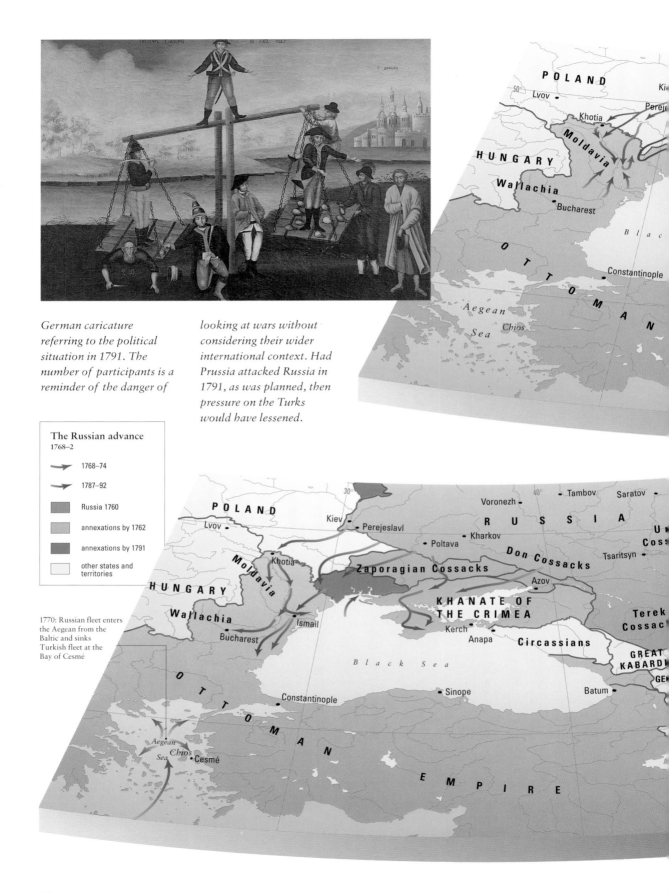

German caricature referring to the political situation in 1791. The number of participants is a reminder of the danger of looking at wars without considering their wider international context. Had Prussia attacked Russia in 1791, as was planned, then pressure on the Turks would have lessened.

The Russian advance
1768–2

→ 1768–74

→ 1787–92

Russia 1760

annexations by 1762

annexations by 1791

other states and territories

1770: Russian fleet enters the Aegean from the Baltic and sinks Turkish fleet at the Bay of Cesmé

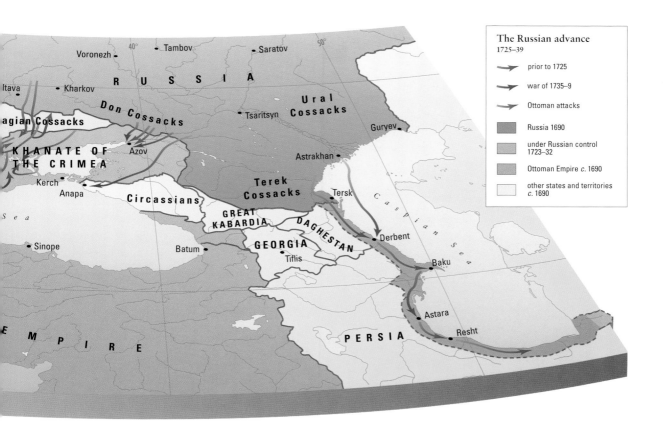

After a bombardment, General Münnich, the German-born head of the Russian war ministry, ordered an attack by night, in columns, against the western section of the lines. The troops climbed the wall and gained control with few losses. The Russians then invaded the Crimea, but its Tartar inhabitants avoided battle and the Russians, debilitated by disease and heat, retreated. Further Russian invasions of the Crimea in 1737 and 1738 were also unsuccessful.

Disease, logistical problems and the scorched earth policies of the Tartars greatly limited Russian successes to the north of the Black Sea in 1737 and 1738, but in 1739 they successfully invaded Bessarabia and Moldavia, defeating the Turks at Stavuchanakh and capturing Khotin and Iasi.

In the Russo-Turkish war of 1768–74 Count Peter Rumyantsev was similarly successful at the head of Russian armies in 1770 and 1774, although his offensive in 1773 was less so. He abandoned traditional linear tactics and, instead, organized his infantry into columns that could advance rapidly and independently, and re-form into hollow divisional squares while affording

THE RUSSIAN ADVANCE

The Russians found the Turkish empire a more formidable foe than Sweden or Poland. Nevertheless, by 1739 they had devised a successful offensive system and were to win repeated victories in the wars of 1768–74 and 1787–92.

mutual support in concerted attacks. The columns relied on fire-power to repel Ottoman assaults and included mobile light artillery. A major role was also played by bayonet charges: fire-power was followed by hand-to-hand fighting. In this way, the mobility of Turkish cavalry, which so threatened forces deployed in a linear fashion by turning their flanks, had been overcome. These tactics prefigured those of the forces of Revolutionary France.

Rumyantsev's tactics helped to bring success in battles such as Ryabaya Mogila, Larga and Kagul in 1770 and Kozludji in 1774. Ottoman casualties were far greater than those of the Russians: at Larga 3,000 Ottomans to fewer than 100 Russians, at Kagul 20,000 to 1,470. At Kozludji (9 June 1774) the Russian square advanced and beat off a janissary attack supported by Baron Tott's batteries. Rain spoiled the cartridges in the cloth pockets of the janissaries; the Russians, who used leather pockets, were more fortunate. Russian fire-power was supported by a cavalry attack that broke the Turkish will to fight; twenty-five of Tott's cannon were captured. The Crimea was overrun in 1771

Prince Gregory Potemkin (1739–91). A lover of Catherine the Great, he became a Field Marshal and pushed Russian development of the Ukraine and expansion towards the Black Sea. Potemkin was in command in the storming of Ochakov in 1788 and the advance to the Dniester in 1789.

and the Ottoman fortress system on the Danube was breached in 1770 and 1774.

Success was more than a matter of battlefield skill and determination. The Russian army was also increasingly expert in the deployment of their forces. The adoption of more flexible means of supply helped to reduce the cumbersome baggage trains, although logistics remained a serious problem until the development of railways in the nineteenth century, not least because of the, by modern standards, primitive nature of the empire's administrative system. However, improvements permitted better strategic planning, including better use of riverine and littoral communications. Aware of the logistical difficulties faced by a large army, Rumyantsev grasped the need to take the initiative. By the Treaty of Kutchuk-Kainardji of 1774, the Russians gained territory to the north of the Black Sea, including the coast as far as the Dniester.

The Russians were also successful against the Turks in their next conflict, in 1787–92, although the war was hard fought. In the first battle, the Russians defeated a Turkish force that had landed near Kinburn (2 October 1787); it took

Russian defeat over the Turks at Cesmé, 1770. This victory, primarily due to the effective use of fireships against the closely-moored Turkish fleet, was part of a pattern of Russian naval success over the Turks.

nine hours for the Russians under Count Alexander Suvorov to prevail, after bitter hand-to-hand fighting against troops supported by Turkish warships.

In 1788 the Russians moved on to the attack, focusing on the powerful fortress of Ochakov, which overlooked the entrance to the Bug and the Dnieper. Catherine's favourite and former lover, Prince Gregory Potemkin, led the besieging army, and bitter naval engagements took place offshore as the Russians struggled to create an effective blockade. After lengthy bombardment, Ochakov was stormed on 17 December. In 1789 the main Russian army under Potemkin, advanced to the Dniester; in 1790 the forts in the Danube delta, such as Izmail, were captured and in 1791 the Russians advanced south of the Danube. The victories in the wars of 1768–74 and 1787–92 established Russia on the Black Sea, gained her the Crimea (taken in 1783), pushed the Turkish frontier back to the Balkans and challenged the Turkish position there.

Fire-power and determination were also crucial in the Kuban, to the east of the Black Sea. When, in 1783, the Nogais resisted being incorporated into the expanding Russian state, 3,000 of them were killed at the battle of Urai-Ilgasi, in August, by a small, disciplined force under Suvorov; and, on 2 October, in another battle at the confluence of the Kuban and the River Laba, Suvorov again inflicted heavy casualties. The ability to force battles on nomadic and semi-nomadic peoples was crucial to their defeat.

The Russians were less successful further east, because their targets were more distant, they devoted far fewer military resources to the task and there were no communication routes along the rivers as there had been in the Ukraine. The major initiative was taken by Peter the Great, ever one to test the frontiers of the possible. In a campaign that depended on logistics as much as on battles, Peter advanced along the Caspian Sea in 1722–3. He hoped to benefit from the disintegration of Persia at Afghan hands to gain control of the silk routes, annex territory and pre-empt Ottoman expansion. Derbent fell in 1722, Baku and Rasht in 1723. This was not the advance of a cavalry army, such as that of the Afghans, but rather a more systematic enterprise mostly involving infantry. It was characterized by attempts to create a permanent military imprint by, for example, the construction or improvement of forts and roads, so as to anchor and sustain any Russian presence. This, however, proved to be a campaign too far. The Russians found that their gains to the west and south of the Caspian were of little use. Large numbers of garrison troops, possibly as many as 130,000 men, were lost through disease and, at a time of Persian revival under Nadir Shah, the lands to the south of the Caspian were ceded by the Russians in 1732. Although in the nineteenth and twentieth centuries the Russians would occupy parts of northern Persia on occasion, their best opportunity for creating a territorial presence there had been lost. Russia was not to benefit from the collapse of the Safavid empire – as Britain did from the collapse of Mughal power in India – and would face more resilient Persian governments thereafter.

The Russians had more success to the east of the Caspian, an important, but overlooked, sphere of European expansion in this period. Again, it was a case of logistics and consolidation rather than of battle. The Bashkirs were suppressed to the north-east of the Caspian in the 1720s and 1730s. Local allies were the most effective in suppressing resistance. Russian control was anchored by a new line of forts from the Volga to Orenburg. Other lines of forts consolidated their advancing frontiers, defying the Dsungars and the Kalmyks. The southward advances of these fortifications paralleled the offensive tactics of Russian infantry and artillery. They also sealed off regions from hostile reinforcement. The way was closed for nomadic invasions and the ground prepared for subsequent Russian advances into Kazakhstan and central Asia.

The Russians did not always succeed, however. An expedition sent to persuade the Khan of Khiva in central Asia to accept Russian suzerainty, and then to investigate the route to India, was annihilated in 1717. The entrenched Russians beat off attacks for two days, but were tricked into leaving their position and were massacred. Another expedition, sent to discover gold sands in Dsungaria, was defeated in 1719. However, these were very far-flung enterprises. The strength of Russia's southern frontiers and the steady pressure of Russian power in a part of the world traditionally characterized by the advances of steppe peoples was more impressive.

The demographics of warfare were very different in south Asia. Here European forces were heavily outnumbered and there were no settlement colonies – as there had been in North and South America and along the frontiers of Austrian and Russian advance – to provide local militias and manpower; the Europeans could only operate successfully if they recruited local ancillaries, a process begun in India by the Portuguese in the early sixteenth century. Furthermore, the political context of European expansion in south Asia was also very different to the situation in the New World and in the zones of Austrian and Russian advance. In general, especially in the first half of the century, the Europeans were not seeking territorial expansion but simply wanted to ensure that the local system of politics favoured the profitability of their trade. However, competition with other European powers and ambition for territorial gain encouraged expansionism in some contexts, especially with the British in India from 1757.

European military activity in India in the eighteenth century is usually discussed in terms of the impressive achievements of Robert Clive, later Lord Clive (1725–74), first in the Carnatic (south-east India) and then in Bengal, where he defeated the Nawab, Siraj-ud-daula, at Plassey on 23 June 1757. However, it is important to note that such successes were atypical. There was no European military pressure on China, Japan or Siam in the eighteenth century, which represented a total failure to follow up on the bold plans of conquest advanced in the sixteenth century. The general pattern was of limited activity and only limited results: the Spaniards had scant success in subduing and Christianizing the southern Philippines; British and French attempts to establish a presence in

INDIA IN THE
EIGHTEENTH CENTURY

*The military history of
India in this period needs to
be seen not only in terms of
British expansion, but also
with reference to struggles
between Indian powers as
well as their response to
expansionist non-European
rulers.*

southern Burma failed; the Persian Gulf remained closed to European power. French arms and advisers played a role in Vietnam from the late 1780s, but to the benefit of the expansionist schemes of Nguyen Anh, who had conquered all Vietnam by 1802 and proclaimed himself Emperor Gia-Long, rather than in order to advance French control.

The increasing prominence of the British among the European presence in south Asia was to some extent a measure of the failure there of the other European powers. In the case of the French this was largely due to their defeats in India at the hands of the British, especially in 1760–61; but in the case of the Dutch and Portuguese this was not only due to general problems of their no longer being great powers, but also to specific defeats at the hands of Asian states. Thus the Portuguese were hard-pressed in India in 1737–40 when they were involved in a disastrous war with the Marathas; Salsette, Bassein and Chaul were captured and they very nearly lost their major base, Goa. As a consequence, the British, based in Bombay, became the dominant European power in west India.

The Dutch had been the most dynamic European power in the Indian Ocean

*Robert Clive receiving
money from the Nawab of
Bengal. The ability of
European generals to profit
from conflict was most fully
shown in transoceanic
expansion, not least in India
where British governmental
control over the East India
Company was limited. Clive
established the British
position in Bengal and
Bihar, which provided a
solid source of revenue and
manpower, and was to form
the basis of British imperial
power in Asia.*

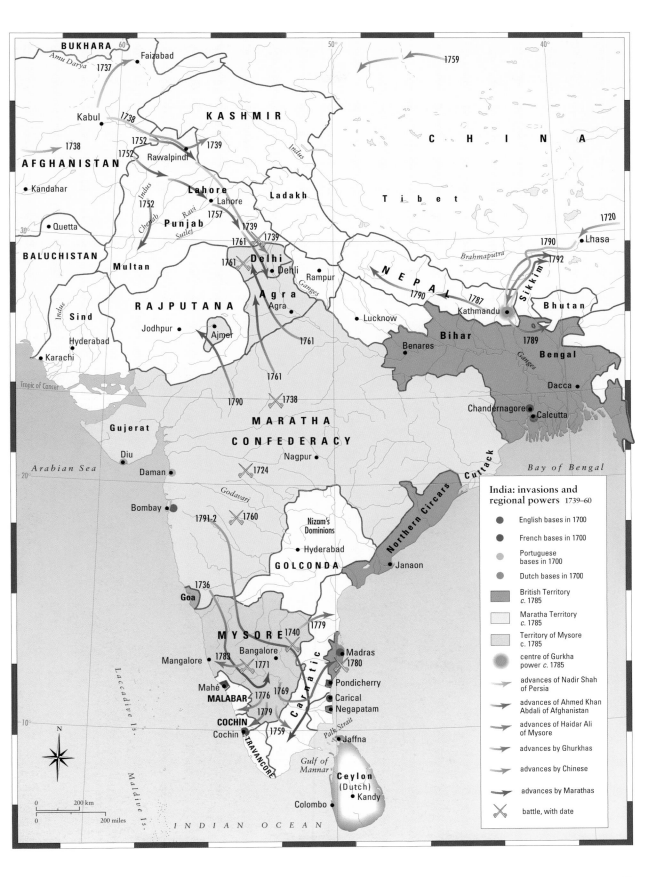

BUKHARA

Amu Darya

60°

• Faizabad

1737

• Kabul

1738

1738

AFGHANISTAN

• Kandahar

30°

• Quetta

BALUCHISTAN

KASHMIR

1752

1738

1752

Rawalpindi

1739

LAHORE

• Lahore

1752

1757

Punjab

Indus

Chenab

Ravi

Sutlej

1739

Ladakh

Indus

50°

1759

40°

C H I N A

T i b e t

1720

1790

• Lhasa

1792

Sikkim

Brahmaputra

1790

1787

N E P A L

Kathmandu

Bhutan

1789

1761

1739

1739

Delhi

1761

• Dehli

Agra

• Agra

Rampur

Ganges

Multan

Sind

• Hyderabad

• Karachi

Indus

Tropic of Cancer

RAJPUTANA

Jodhpur •

• Ajmer

1761

1761

1790

1738

• Lucknow

Benares •

Bihar

Bengal

Ganges

• Dacca

Chandernagore

• Calcutta

20°

Arabian Sea

Gujerat

Diu •

Daman •

Bombay •

1724

M A R A T H A

C O N F E D E R A C Y

Nagpur •

Godavari

1791-2

1760

Nizam's
Dominions

• Hyderabad

G O L C O N D A

Northern Circars

Cuttack

Bay of Bengal

• Janaon

MYSORE

1736

Goa

1740

1779

Bangalore •

1783

Mangalore •

1771

Mahé •

MALABAR

1776

1769

1779

COCHIN

Cochin •

1759

TRAVANCORE

Madras

1780

Carnatic

Pondicherry

Carical

Negapatam

Palk Strait

• Jaffna

*Gulf of
Mannar*

Ceylon
(Dutch)

• Kandy

Colombo •

Laccadive Is.

Maldive Is.

N

0   200 km

0   200 miles

10°

I N D I A N   O C E A N

India: invasions and
regional powers 1739–60

● English bases in 1700

● French bases in 1700

● Portuguese
bases in 1700

● Dutch bases in 1700

British Territory
c. 1785

Maratha Territory
c. 1785

Territory of Mysore
c. 1785

● centre of Gurkha
power *c.* 1785

→ advances of Nadir Shah
of Persia

→ advances of Ahmed Khan
Abdali of Afghanistan

→ advances of Haidar Ali
of Mysore

→ advances by Ghurkhas

→ advances by Chinese

→ advances by Marathas

✕ battle, with date

British commanders in India such as Coote and Cornwallis stressed the importance of bullocks for moving the artillery. Cornwallis, and later Wellesley, were helped by the appearance of brinjaries, Indian entrepreneurs who hired out bullocks and sold rice. Cornwallis's advance on Seringapatam in 1791 was hit by an epidemic among the bullocks and, as a result, he had to abandon many of the cannon.

in the seventeenth century, but the situation was very different in the eighteenth century. In Java, the Dutch East India Company's interventions in the persistent civil wars in the kingdom of Mataram were weakened by the inability of the Dutch army to operate successfully away from the coastal areas, not least because of the absence of naval support. More generally, the effectiveness of the Dutch in Java depended on local allies. When in 1741 the Dutch were hard-pressed and their coastal headquarters at Sĕmarang was besieged by an estimated 23,500 Javanese and local Chinese, supported by thirty cannon, their position was saved by an agreement with Cakraningrat IV of Madura, whose forces were crucial to Dutch operations in the interior. But when Pakubuwana II of Mataram reached terms with the Dutch in 1743, a dissatisfied Cakraningrat began a war with them. The balance of military and political advantage was always shifting, and any unexpected pressure could lead to crisis. As a consequence, in the Third Javanese War of Succession (1746–57), the Dutch suffered defeats in 1750 and 1755, while in the kingdom of Banten in west Java, a rebellion in 1750 led to the defeat of Dutch forces. The Dutch East India Company was far weaker than its British counterpart. Its profits fell in the

1730s, 1740s and 1750s, ending the earlier programme of long-term expansion; attempts to reassert their power in the 1740s and 1750s were generally unsuccessful. On Sulawesi, a Dutch attempt in 1739–40 to crush the dynamic Arung Singkang, ruler of Wajo, had only limited success. Disease and bad weather greatly hindered the Dutch.

The Dutch adopted a hesitant role in the Malay world, not least because of

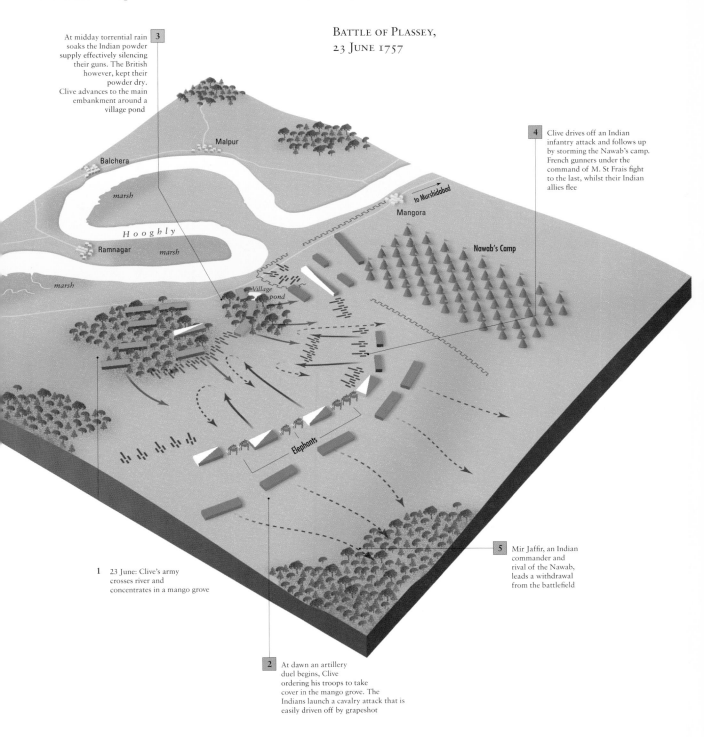

BATTLE OF PLASSEY,
23 JUNE 1757

3 At midday torrential rain soaks the Indian powder supply effectively silencing their guns. The British however, kept their powder dry. Clive advances to the main embankment around a village pond

4 Clive drives off an Indian infantry attack and follows up by storming the Nawab's camp. French gunners under the command of M. St Frais fight to the last, whilst their Indian allies flee

Malpur

Balchera

marsh

Hooghly

Ramnagar   *marsh*

marsh

to Murshidabad

Mangora

Nawab's Camp

Village pond

Elephants

5 Mir Jaffir, an Indian commander and rival of the Nawab, leads a withdrawal from the battlefield

1 23 June: Clive's army crosses river and concentrates in a mango grove

2 At dawn an artillery duel begins, Clive ordering his troops to take cover in the mango grove. The Indians launch a cavalry attack that is easily driven off by grapeshot

concern over the contrast between their weak defences in Malacca and the military strength of the expanding Bugis, although the Bugi siege of Malacca was to be repelled in 1784. Far from there being a tide of European advance, there were no important Dutch operations in the Malay world, after a punitive expedition against Siak in 1761, until 1784.

In India, the Dutch were defeated by Travancore in 1741. In 1761–6 they faced a difficult war in Sri Lanka that indicated the limitations of the European military. Far from the war beginning with an act of European aggression, it was launched not by the Dutch, but by Kirti Sri, the ruler of the interior kingdom of Kandy. Exploiting discontent in the militarily weak Dutch coastal possessions, he attacked and overran much of the coast. As elsewhere, however, where European power was attacked, for example in North America during Pontiac's War in 1763–4, it proved far harder for the indigenous forces to capture fortified positions and Dutch-led Negombo successfully resisted attack in 1761. Furthermore, the Europeans benefited from their ability to deploy troops from elsewhere in the European world. The Dutch sent reinforcements, many from the East Indies, and by the end of 1763 they had regained the coastal regions.

Soldier of Tipu Sultan of Mysore armed with flintlock. Mysore proved to be especially adept at adopting European-style fire-power tactics and seriously threatened the British position in the Carnatic.

In 1764 the Dutch set out to take the interior. Six columns were sent against the capital, but they were as unsuccessful in this as the much earlier Portuguese expeditions into the interior in 1594, 1630 and 1638. There had been no improvement in European offensive military capability; the usual problems of operating in the tropics, particularly disease, difficult terrain and an absence of maps, were exacerbated by Kandyan resistance. Taking advantage of the jungle terrain, Kandyan sharpshooters harassed the Dutch, inflicting heavy casualties.

Learning from past mistakes was an important characteristic of successful European operations. In January 1765 the Dutch launched a new campaign, replacing swords and bayonets with less cumbersome machetes, providing a more practical uniform and moving more rapidly. To begin with, the Dutch triumphed, capturing the deserted capital, but the Kandyans refused to engage in battle – always a sensible response to European fire-power. This meant that Dutch energies were dissipated in seeking to control a country rendered intractable by disease and enemy raiders. Peace was made in 1766. Kandy would not be conquered until the British overran it in 1815.

It is helpful to consider British achievements in India in the light of the Dutch failure in Kandy. First, Kirti Sri's attack in 1761 serves as a useful reminder that this was not simply a case of European expansion. Indeed, in India, Clive's advance into Bengal in 1757 followed an attack by the Nawab on Calcutta; in

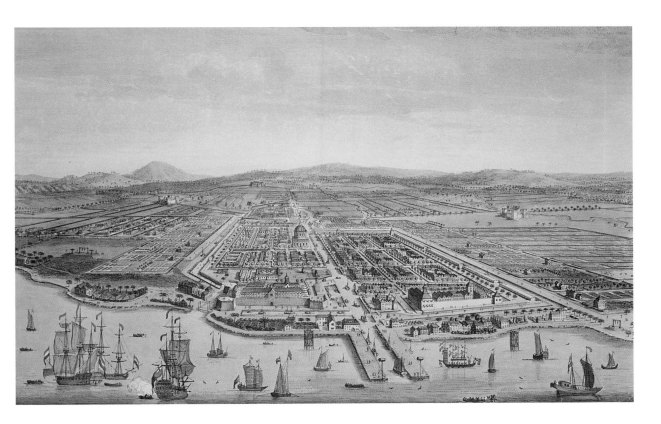

west India the Marathas were a dynamic force; in south India Haidar Ali of Mysore pressed on the British sphere of influence in the Carnatic.

Second, success was not all one way. Alongside the victories through which the British came to dominate Bengal – Plassey (23 June 1757), Patna (3 May 1764) and Buxar (23 October 1764) – and the successful advances on the Mysore capital, Seringapatam, that led Haidar's son, Tipu Sultan, first to yield to British terms (1792) and then to defeat and death (1799), there were also serious failures. In late 1778 a slow-moving army of 3,200 infantry, with 12,000 bullocks pulling arms and supplies, advanced from Bombay into the difficult terrain of the Ghats. The army was not up to the task and failed to master the crucial problems of mobility, logistics and terrain, advancing less than a mile a day. The Marathas made a stand on 9 January 1779, but retreated when the British formed up and advanced. Concerned about communications and a lack of support for their Maratha protégé, the civilian committee with the British army then ordered a retreat, although the commander, Lieutenant Colonel William Cockburn, argued that it would be dangerous to retreat in open country in face of the opposing Maratha forces, especially as the enemy cavalry moved very rapidly. In the event, Cockburn's force was quickly surrounded by a far larger force. On 12 January he wrote, 'we remained under a severe cannonade, having the whole flower of the Maratha horse ready to charge whenever an opportunity offered, but our well served artillery and the steadiness of the infantry prevented them'. By the following night, however, the army was badly affected by failing morale;

Batavia, the major Dutch base in the East Indies, c. 1780, when a Dutch squadron was based there. Jayakerta had been captured by the Dutch in 1619 and renamed Jakarta.

Bronze mortar, made for Tipu Sultan of Mysore, c. 1790. Asian artillery was more varied than its European counterparts. Animal motifs accentuated the symbolic power of artillery.

desertions sapped its strength and ammunition supplies were falling. The British signed a convention at Wadgaon, agreeing to withdraw to Bombay. A well-trained force could only achieve so much, especially if on difficult terrain in the face of considerably more numerous opponents and if reconnaissance was inadequate.

Mysore's armies defeated British forces in 1780 and 1782. Mysore also had effective light cavalry. The British advance on Seringapatam in 1791 failed: having reached the city, defeating a Mysore force outside it, the British found themselves short of supplies and with the monsoon about to break, before a strongly fortified position. They fell back in disorder, abandoning many of their cannon.

Individual successes and failures had different causes, but the overall lesson was that Indian military systems were not foredoomed to failure. The British found it easier to confront opponents who relied primarily on infantry, but the Marathas and Mysore both depended on light cavalry. In 1768, when the East India Company was at war with Mysore, a British officer wrote of 'a large body of the enemy's horse constantly hovering about us, and often carrying away numbers of our bullocks, baggage, etc.'. Short of cavalry, the Company's forces could not respond effectively. Lord Cornwallis, the British commander-in-chief in India, wrote in 1787, 'no man in India can be more convinced than I am of the importance of cavalry to our armies'.

The light cavalry of Britain's opponents could best be thwarted only if the British recruited local allies. Hence their reliance on sepoys – Indian infantry trained to fight with the weapons and tactics of their European counterparts – and on Indian cavalry campaigning in their own units. The British use of allied Indian military forces went back to Stringer Lawrence in the Carnatic in the 1740s, and put a premium on the political skill of British leaders, on the financial resources of Britain's Indian possessions, and also on the factors encouraging Indian rulers to help Britain. Thus the 1792 and 1799 advances on Seringapatam were more successful than that of 1791 largely because local allies had been secured. The failure of Hyderabad, Mysore and the Marathas to make common cause against the British was crucial. Similarly, the British victory at Plassey in 1757 owed much to dissension in the army of the Nawab of Bengal; in addition, the Nawab had to divide his forces in order to meet a possible Afghan attack.

This political dimension of warfare repeats the experience of earlier episodes of European expansion – Cortes against the Aztecs in sixteenth-century Mexico for example, and also of warfare within Europe. There, too, shifting alliances were a vital context and adjunct of war. Politics were also involved in the cohesion of opposing states. Like China, the European powers had great strength as a result of the continuity of administrative organization and governmental identity. Opponents that were largely dependent on the leadership of a single individual were weaker. In 1783 John Kennaway, a British soldier in India, observed that the death of Haidar Ali in 1782:

has occasioned a very sensible change in the face of our affairs: but such excellent order had that extraordinary man established in the civil and military departments of his government that contrary to what we have usually seen and read of on the death of an Asiatic Prince, since the decline of the Mogul Empire, his son though engaged on a distant expedition succeeded with as little disturbance as if it had been to an ancient and hereditary kingdom. The charm however was dissolved. Haidar's name with the different powers [of India] operated with the force of magic and though Tipu may be equal in abilities to his father he must be as well known before he can be equally respected.

The British did not only have to consider alliances with native powers in India. Such alliances were also important in North America, where there was no intermediary to the power of the British government equivalent to the East India Company. There again the general impression of European military superiority and territorial expansion has to be supplemented by an awareness of the setbacks that were faced and of the often complex reasons for European success. In North America all the expanding European powers – Britain from the eastern seaboard, France from New France (Québec) and Louisiana, Spain from the frontier of settlement north of Mexico and in Florida, and Russia in the Aleutian Islands and Alaska – encountered problems, although none which prevented the extension of political power and territorial control or influence. This pattern was to be continued by the newly independent United States, although the pace of expansion was pushed far more strongly and continuously than under the European powers and was far more closely linked with the growing population and with a major extension of the cultivated area.

Initially in the eighteenth century France was the European power that expanded most vigorously in North America. Whereas the British colonies were bound more closely to the Atlantic seaboard and to the frontier of settlement, the French projected their power along the great rivers of the interior, especially the Mississippi, following trade routes and seeking to link Québec with New Orleans in a bold imperial undertaking. Much of this expansion was achieved without the use of force. As the French sought trade, not land, an accommodation could often be reached, but when there was resistance they hit hard. In Louisiana in 1729–31 the Natchez were crushed, a campaign of systematic extermination that was helped by the failure of other tribes to assist them. The Fox tribe of Mississippi–Illinois was defeated in what was to be Illinois in 1730. The French suffered defeat at the hands of the Chickasaw in the late 1730s and were hit by Chickasaw raids in 1747–8 and 1752, but their destruction of native villages and crops forced the Chickasaw to terms in 1752. The same year, the Miami, who had sacked Fort Miami in 1747 and Fort Vincennes in 1751, were forced back into alliance: the Miami chief, Memeskia, was killed and eaten in a raid on Pickawillany village. This account of conflict is somewhat misleading as it ignores the general ability of the French to maintain their position without war, an ability that would have been enhanced had the British not stirred up opposition, as with the Miami. In South America the French developed a base at Cayenne in the 1760s.

The Spaniards encountered more resistance in North America than the French, possibly because their advance was linked more closely with settlement. They had been forced out of the Santa Fé region of New Mexico between 1680 and 1692 by the Pueblo rebellion, and were hard pressed there again in the 1770s. In 1751 the Pimas of Arizona rebelled and in 1781 the successful Yuma rebellion thwarted Spanish plans for expansion through the Colorado valley and into central Arizona. The Spaniards faced what they, but not their opponents, saw as rebellion, and also pressure from tribes on the Great Plains moving south, especially the Comanche and the Utes. Well mounted and armed with French firearms, tribes such as the Apache were able to thwart the Spanish expeditions sent against them, for example, in 1732, in 1759 and in 1775. In 1776 there were only 1,900 Spanish troops to defend an 1,800-mile frontier of Spanish North America.

Fox warrior. The French depended on native co-operation in North America. They traded extensively, while their settlements relied on local allies, such as the Choctaws. Agreements and alliances, in turn, drew the French into local rivalries, for example supporting the Potawatomi against the Fox, who were nearly wiped out by French–native attacks in 1712–34.

A successful Spanish attack on the Comanches in 1779 was followed by treaties with them in 1785–6; peace was now the Spanish goal and they used goods and trade to lure the Native Americans. Once they were allied with the Comanches, the Spaniards pressed the Apaches hard; in the 1790s they persuaded many of them to settle on 'peace establishments', the precursors of the later reservations.

The Aleuts of the Aleutian Isles initially posed few problems to the Russians in their quest for furs, but in 1761 effective resistance on the Fox Islands began. However, this was overcome in 1766 by an amphibious force deploying cannon. As earlier in Siberia, massacre and disease secured the Russian 'achievement'. The Tlingits of Alaska were more tenacious foes, partly because they had acquired firearms from British and American traders and partly because in this situation the Russians had little advantage from the naval power that they had used against their island opponents. In 1802 the Tlingits destroyed the Russian base of New Archangel on Sitka.

The British colonies successfully overcame native resistance in some areas,

New Orleans, capital of the French colony at Louisiana, 1719. Hopes that Louisiana would be a breadbasket for the French empire, a mineral colony, or would serve as a base for trade with the Pacific or New Mexico were not realized. Attempts to encourage immigration had scant success, and the Natchez rising in 1729 hit the profitability of the colony. The brutal response included the burning of prisoners alive.

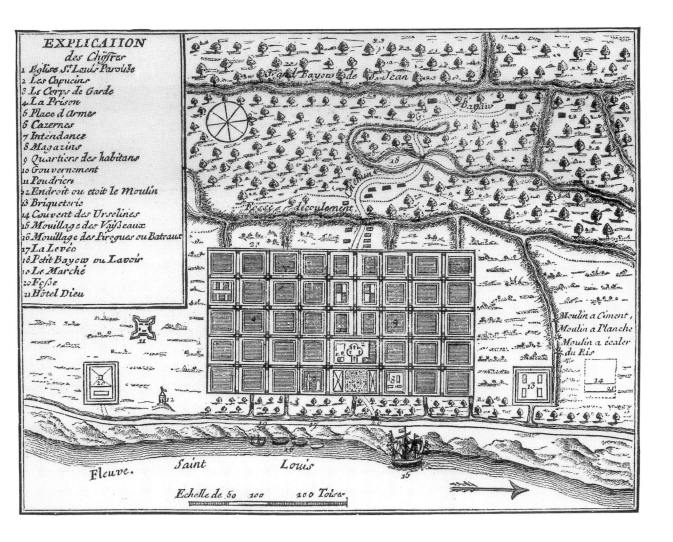

but faced a prolonged struggle in others. Thus, in the 1710s, in the Carolinas, the Yamasee and the Tuscaroras were defeated, from the 1720s the Abenaki kept settlers out of what was to be Vermont and in 1760–61 the Cherokee proved a formidable foe in North Carolina. The most powerful riposte was mounted in Pontiac's War of 1763–4: minor British posts south of the Great Lakes were overrun and British units ambushed, but the major fortified positions – Detroit, Niagara and Fort Pitt (Pittsburg) – held, and, in 1764, the British counter-offensive drove the Native Americans to terms.

As in India, there is no simple explanation for success in some conflicts and failure in others, but some of the most important factors were clearly alliances and the role of alternative commitments. Thus, in the 1710s, far from the natives allying, the Yamasee helped the Carolinians against the Tuscaroras in 1711 and in 1715 the Cherokee assisted them against the Yamasee. For that reason, the widespread nature of Pontiac's War was a threat, but it proved difficult to sustain co-operation, which is not surprising given the vast area at stake. Furthermore, many important tribes did not take part in the rising. The tribes in west Florida, where British power was weak and newly established, neither joined nor imitated the rising. The governor there, George Johnstone, took care to seek Native American support.

The failure of the Native Americans to co-operate was particularly important when and where the Europeans lacked numbers, as in west Florida. This was generally the case in frontier zones and in areas of new settlement. By the end of 1720 the population of the French colony of Louisiana was only about 4,000, including nearly 1,000 soldiers. Such numbers explain why winning the support of Native American allies was so important. The newly established Spanish base on Vancouver Island was not attacked in 1790–91 because of rivalries between the local bands and their desire to trade with the Spaniards. There were, however, minor clashes. Twice Spanish launches were repelled; the second time, arrows were countered by muskets and swivel guns, and the light artillery of the launches made a dramatic impact.

The hostility of other European powers could be serious. Thus, the French provided the Abenaki with arms and ammunition for use against the British. However, once the French had been driven from Canada the arms supply ceased , placing the Native Americans at a disadvantage in Pontiac's War. Thus, native superiority in fighting in the varied environments of North America, particularly in woodcraft, was not matched by their political and logistical resources.

In the closing decades of the period the situation deteriorated for Native Americans both on the Pacific littoral and in the 'Old North-west', the lands south of the Great Lakes. In the former, Spanish advances in coastal California from 1769, Russian pressure in Alaska and the British presence in what was to be British Columbia were all either dependent on, or assisted by, command of the sea. As so often across the world in this period, this could not be challenged effectively by non-Europeans; European powers were able to apply direct military pressure from the sea and, more significantly, support their forces and integrate new acquisitions into global trading networks, making the process of advance both possible and profitable. This was crucial to the Russian quest for furs, first in the Aleutians, then in Alaska and, finally, down the coast towards California.

Further east, many Native Americans had supported the British during the American War of Independence and they had not been defeated or outfought. The frontier of European settlement had been pressed hard, particularly in New York and Pennsylvania in 1778. The natives maintained the initiative at the close of the war, defeating the American Patriots in Kentucky and on the shores of Lake Erie in 1782. Expeditions by the Patriots, such as John Sullivan's campaign against the Iroquois in 1779, were often unsuccessful, in Sullivan's case in large part because of the logistical problems facing expeditions deep into the interior, especially a lack of transport. Nevertheless, thanks to careful reconnaissance, Sullivan's army was able to avoid ambush.

The native forces were militarily sophisticated. The rank and file were disciplined and led by capable officers. Their battlefield manoeuvring made expert use of flanking movements proceeding from a half-moon starting position. These movements could be used for advance or retreat. However, despite their fighting quality, the cumulative pressure of sustained conflict damaged native society and disrupted their economies. In 1779 Sullivan destroyed many villages and 160,000 bushels of corn, causing much suffering.

Furthermore, the lessening of British support after American independence left Native Americans more vulnerable when the pressure and pace of settlement accelerated. The importance of foreign support was shown in 1786 when the Creeks of Alabama and Mississippi used arms supplied by Spanish governors to repel the westward advance of Georgians. However, in 1795 Spain accepted the thirty-first parallel as the northern border of west Florida, opening the way for American penetration into the lands of the south-eastern tribes.

Despite some successes, including the victory of the Miamis under Little Turtle on the Maumee river in western Ohio (18–22 October 1790) and the defeat of Arthur St Clair's army on the Wabash river in Ohio (4 November 1791), the Native Americans found it difficult to cope with the casualties and consequences of defeat. The native position in the 'Old North-west' was broken by Anthony Wayne's victory at the battle of Fallen Timbers on 20 August 1794, a victory that allowed expansion into the region. An American bayonet charge played a crucial role in this victory. The natives were malnourished and, in part, taken by surprise, and they were also affected by a withdrawal of British support.

The American advance was consolidated by their victories in the 1810s over tribes with close ties to the British in Canada: the Shawnees at Tippecanoe in 1811 and at the battle of the Thames (near London, Ontario) in 1813. Further south, the Creeks were attacked in 1813 and defeated at Tallasahatchee (3 November) and Talladega (9 November). The following year, Andrew Jackson

OPPOSITE: *Surinam Carib. Britain, France, Portugal and Spain claimed territory between the Orinoco and Amazon, but their presence was restricted by disease and native resistance. Spain encouraged the use of a slave labour force.*

Brazilian tribesmen. Portuguese expansion into the interior of Brazil led to conflict in which the Portuguese were helped by native disunity, and, indeed, allies. The Muras in Central Amazonia in the 1760s and 1770s made very effective use of bows and arrows in attacks on canoes and isolated settlements. Yet, they could check, but not defeat, the Portuguese.

attacked the centres of Creek power and stormed their fortified camp at Horseshoe Bend (27 March).

South America is generally denied any military history between Pizarro's overthrow of the Incas in the 1530s and the Wars of Liberation in the early nineteenth century. This is misleading. The conquistadors had taken only a fraction of South America, and in succeeding centuries conflict between Spanish and Portuguese colonies and natives continued. In addition, there were rebellions in these colonies and warfare between native groups, while, although this was less common, there was also conflict between the Spaniards and the Portuguese. In some areas, the colonial powers made considerable advances.

This was particularly true in the Portuguese colony of Brazil, where the discovery of goldfields in the interior led to an intensification of European activity and, inevitably, to a native response. The Cuiabá goldfields were discovered in 1719 and the consequences of exploitation soon worried the Native Americans. A convoy of gold seekers in canoes was destroyed by the Paiaguá on the River Paraguay in 1725 and another was mauled the following year. The Paiaguá fired their bows more rapidly than the Portuguese their muskets, and they also made masterly use of their canoes, not least by leaping into the water and tipping them up to protect themselves from musket fire. In 1730 the annual flotilla carrying gold was ambushed and mostly destroyed on the way back from Cuiabá. Punitive expeditions achieved little in 1730 and 1731, but in 1734 the

Iroquois village of the early seventeenth century. Native villages could offer effective opposition. Their reliance on simple palisade designs matched that of European forts in the interior of North America. In contrast, European coastal positions such as Charleston, Louisbourg and St Augustine designed to resist European-style sieges were far more formidable.

combination of surprise attack and fire-power devastated the Paiaguá. Although the Paiaguá mounted successful attacks in 1735 and 1736, their casualties led to a slackening of activity and they were also affected by disease and by the attacks of the Guaicurú Indians. By the 1780s the Paiaguá had been largely wiped out, but their story shows the danger of assuming a simple model of European military superiority. Elsewhere, the use of native allies was important: Portuguese troops were unable to defeat the Caiapó, who ambushed Portuguese settlements and convoys, but the Bororo, under the leadership of a Portuguese woodsman António Pires de Campos, pressed them hard in a bitter war between 1745 and 1751.

The ability to win and exploit local allies reflected the lack of native unity. (The situation had been the same when the Turks attacked Europe in the fifteenth and sixteenth centuries.) This, disease and the consequences of enslavement all helped the Portuguese far more than any particular success in contact warfare. Portuguese fire-power was important but natives such as the Muras in central Amazonia learned to avoid it.

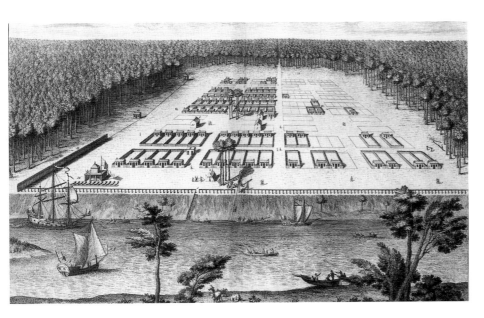

Founded in 1733 by James Oglethorpe, Savannah was the principal position in the British colony of Georgia. As with Charleston, its defences were intended against Spain, not the native population. In relations with Spain the Georgia–Florida border issue was vexed. In 1779 the British garrison successfully resisted an American– French attack.

The Muras, adept with their bows and arrows, and effective owing to their mobility, harried Portuguese settlements and trade routes in the 1760s and 1770s, but they could only check, not reverse, the tide of advance. The same was true of native resistance to the Spaniards (on the Mosquito Coast of Nicaragua, in the Guajiro Peninsula in Colombia in the 1770s and by the Araucanians in Chile) and to the British (by the Maroons, runaway slaves, in the interior of Jamaica in the 1730s and by the native Caribs on the West Indian island of St Vincent).

European control was anchored by fortifications, for example those along the Bío Bío river in Chile, such as the fortress of Nacimiento, or the Spanish fortress at Pensacola in western Florida founded in 1698, or that at Monterey, established in 1770 as the capital of New California. Similarly, in India the British developed powerful fortresses at Bombay, Calcutta and Madras. When George Paterson visited Bombay in 1770 he thought the square fort in which the British had sheltered against the Mughals in 1686 'by no means fit to sustain a modern attack', but noted more modern fortifications going up, including those on a hill overlooking the town. He was greatly impressed by the speed of the work:

> it must be fortified. Well this being agreed to, the fortifications were well planned and immediately carried into execution, and all the time they were employed about this, there were several thousands also constantly at work to take away the hill and blowing it up like fire and smoke. They both come on apace and very soon there will be no hill; but there will be fine fortifications ... All these works put together may be very well defended by 10,000 men, an army sufficient to meet any power in the field that can attack this place; but one may as well fight under cover as not.

'Am I not a man and your brother.' An anti-slavery slogan on an enamelled snuff box from Switzerland, made in the late eighteenth century, probably 1790. Slavery was in part a by-product of warfare between African states.

As with Spanish *presidios* and Russian lines of fortifications, this was part of the process in which the European presence rested on the ability to dig. In 1788 Lord Cornwallis, the British commander in India, took an interest in the purchase of entrenching tools. Having already ordered '4,000 good iron shovels', he wanted '2,000 iron spades to be made immediately'.

However, due to a lack of interest and resources, many fortified positions were weak and poorly garrisoned. In 1710 the wood of the French fortress at Fort Louis (later Mobile), which had been built in 1702, was so rotted by humidity and decay that it could not support the weight of the cannon. The garrison suffered from an absence of fresh meat, from an insufficient supply of swords, cartridge boxes, nails, guns and powder, from demoralization and desertion, and from the lack of a hospital. The survival of Louisiana at that stage rested on its acceptance by the native population; European imperialism there, as in many other places, can be described as much in terms of mutual benefit and consensus, as of the coercive cutting edge of military superiority.

The Europeans held no monopoly of fortifications. For example, eastern Native Americans had many palisaded villages in the seventeenth century and, with the introduction of firearms, European-style bastions appeared to defend against cross-fire. There was at least one example of a masonry fort in New England. However, the Native Americans usually abandoned their forts when Europeans approached them, particularly when the latter had cannon. They had learned that forts could be death traps.

Powerful European-colonial fortifications were of limited use against European assailants who had naval superiority and were not weakened by tropical diseases, as the British demonstrated when they took Louisbourg on Cape Breton Island from the French in 1745 and, for good, in 1758. However, such fortifications were generally able to resist assailants who lacked the skills, resources and organization required for a lengthy siege, and in the eighteenth century most major fortifications erected by European forces survived native siege or attack. In north Africa, Spanish-held Ceuta resisted Moroccan sieges in the period 1694–1720 and in 1732, and Melilla another in 1774–5. On the other hand, the Algerians took Oran from Spain in 1708, and the Dahomians succeeded in capturing the Portuguese fort at Whydah in 1727 and 1743, the second time through fire igniting stores of gunpowder. The Portuguese also lost Mombasa to the Omani Arabs in 1698 and again (after retaking it in 1728) in 1729, and Mazagan to Morocco in 1765. In 1729 the besiegers of

Mombasa had no artillery and very few firearms, but the garrison surrendered as a result of low morale and problems with food supplies. A Portuguese attempt to regain Mombasa in 1769 failed.

However, these losses were by European powers that were weak at that time. This was true of Portugal and, in 1708, of Spain, then greatly debilitated by the War of the Spanish Succession. The major centres of European power did not fall to non-European peoples. Spanish-ruled Manila fell to the British in 1762, not to a rising in the Philippines or to an attacking Asian power. The Massachusetts forces that captured Louisbourg in 1745 acted like European regulars: the fortress was besieged and its walls breached by cannon. This was not an exercise in wilderness warfare. Native Americans could not have mounted a comparable attack.

Nevertheless, the possession of coastal fortresses by European powers did not bring control over the interior. The French established a base at Fort Dauphin in 1748, but did not conquer Madagascar until the 1890s. This was a matter of political will as well as of military capability; both were important to conquest. The value of warships in support of fortresses was indicated by Captain William Cornwallis, as in his report to the British Admiralty about a voyage to the River Gambia in February 1775:

Upon sending an officer up to James' Fort, I was informed by the commanding officer that the French had spirited the natives up against the English, and that he had been obliged to take a schooner of some force belonging to the traders into the service in order to supply himself with water; I thought the appearance of a man of war might be of service. I therefore went up the river in the *Pallas* to James' Fort, which I found in great distress for want of stores, and particularly gun-carriages, not having above three or four serviceable ones in the Fort, and most of their guns rendered totally useless for want of them ... I stayed in the River eight days, during which time we got the king of the country on board and showed him all the civility we could; he seemed very well pleased, so I hope all will go on well again.

Another decisive factor was resistance: Amerindian resistance to the Europeans was at its most effective when it was 'primitive', especially if aided by difficult terrain or eco-systems, as in tropical forests. When peoples practised dispersed warfare (not, probably, as a result of deep reasoning, but because they were skilled in hunting) against more sophisticated, cohesive, concentrated European formations, they were often successful in frustrating, although rarely in 'beating', them. If the peoples were nomadic or had scattered settlements, they obviously presented the Europeans with fewer or poorer fixed assets to threaten. The British in India found this a fundamental problem: the more sophisticated, 'civilized' peoples were easier to oppress than the 'primitives'. However, the 'primitives' too were generally contained or controlled if it was worthwhile for the Europeans.

Resistance to European advance was difficult, but native rebellion against control that had already been achieved was far harder. In part, this was because rebellion produced economic dislocation and occurred where ethnic solidarity and political practices had already been breached by European conquest and settlement. One of the largest conflicts with the non-European world was the general insurrection in Peru in 1780–81. Provoked by the rigorous collection of taxes, and headed by Túpac Amaru, a descendant of the last Inca rulers, the uprising was crushed. Over 100,000 people died in the conflict. Divisions within the native population played as important a role in this defeat as fire-power.

These factors were also important in limiting slave resistance to European control in North and South America and the West Indies. The whites limited the availability of firearms to slaves. Thus, those plotting what was to be known as Gabriel's Conspiracy in Virginia in 1800, had first to consider how they could acquire guns, horses and swords.

In the New World, as in India and the Balkans, the defeat of non-Western forces had more to do with superior hierarchical command and control in European armies than it had to do with superior weapons, although weapon manufacture, precision and standardization were improving all the time. Chaos usually threatened as soon as battle was joined, but the Europeans kept cohesion and control for longer than their adversaries, permitting more sophisticated tactics in moving or withholding units on the battlefield and more effective fire. These advantages were linked to more general issues of administrative and political capability.

Frontiers of conflict between Europeans and non-Europeans could be found elsewhere, for example in Mozambique. At every point, it is clear that any account of warfare which is restricted only to weaponry or indeed to formal military activity is far too limiting. It is also apparent that any discussion of relations in terms of conflict alone would be unhelpful. Economic, cultural, religious and political ties crossed European/non-European divides, turning them into zones of interaction in which symbiosis, synergy and exchange are analytical terms that are as helpful as conflict and war. Much of the violence across these divides involved an important measure of co-operation; this was especially true of the slave trade, which would not have been possible without the active co-operation of local non-European potentates. Indeed the slave trade encapsulated much of the reality of the European military impact. It was destructive, served the needs of a European-dominated global economy and would have been impossible without local support. It was not until the technological transformations of the nineteenth century – in medicine, communications and fire-power – that the European states would be able to seize territorial control of much more of the world.

CHAPTER THREE

TRANSOCEANIC CONFLICT BETWEEN EUROPEANS

CAPTURE OF LOUISBOURG, 1745. *The best-fortified position in New France, newly built on the Vauban plan, was designed to resist attack from the sea, but was more vulnerable from land, which was where the New Englanders attacked. The fortress surrendered when the walls were breached and the blockading British squadron forced its way into the harbour.*

TRANSOCEANIC CONFLICT BETWEEN EUROPEANS

OPERATING ACROSS THE oceans, European powers were more successful in fighting each other than in conflict with non-Europeans. This was largely because of the dependence of colonial empires on bases and on maritime links with Europe which provided vulnerable targets, and because the units that fought other Europeans were fighting similarly armed and trained forces, even if the environments of conflict were unfamiliar.

Certain areas saw little conflict between the European colonial powers; this was true, for example, of South America, Angola, Mozambique and the South Pacific. Conflict between European powers was concentrated in North America, the West Indies and India. In part, this was a matter of conflict in zones of expansion, as potential benefits were fought over in areas where there was no clear delimitation of authority. Yet other areas of imperial growth, such as the interior of South America, where both Portugal and Spain were expanding, or, in the case of Spain and France, the Louisiana–Texas region, did not produce serious conflict. Similarly, long-established centres of colonial power could be conquered and annexed, as with the British seizure of Québec from the French.

The political context was crucial. Neither Portugal nor the Dutch played a major role in colonial conflict with other European powers in this period. The Dutch defeat of an attack on Kupang in West Timor in 1749 by Portuguese-speaking Christian mestizos based on Flores was not followed by any attempt to overrun Portuguese East Timor; the Dutch lacked the energy and resources. During the Fourth Anglo-Dutch War (1780–84), the security of Dutch positions in Sri Lanka and at Cape Town depended on French support. Trincomalee in Sri Lanka was taken by the British in 1782 but recaptured by the French under Admiral Suffren in the same year. Suffren's arrival also thwarted a planned British attack on Cape Town in 1781; it was not to fall until the next Anglo-Dutch war, in 1795, and then again (having been restored in 1802) in 1806. However, the Dutch base of Negapatam in India fell to the British in 1781, as did their bases on the western coast of Sumatra. Isolated positions were vulnerable to sudden amphibious attack; they tended to lack the support of the hinterland, expensive fortification was incompatible with commercial profit and garrisons were generally small. The Dutch garrison at Yogyakarta in Java was only eighty-nine strong in 1803 and most of these were infirm. In 1781 the Dutch at Batavia on

Java responded to the possibility of British attack by requesting the support of 2,300 troops from the kingdoms of Surakarta and Yogyakarta; there was in fact no attack until 1811, and then Batavia rapidly fell to the British.

Russian expansion in the northern Pacific did not lead to conflict with Britain or Spain. The Russians were greatly hampered by the vast and difficult distances of Siberia and Pacific expansion was very low in their priorities. The Spaniards did not take an active role in the north-east Pacific until late in the century; their naval base at San Blas was not founded until 1768.

Spain generally supported the French, particularly after the Family Compacts of 1733, 1743 and 1761 between their ruling houses. However, there were also colonial tensions between them, especially as a result of French expansion from its newly established colony in Louisiana: Biloxi was founded in 1699 and Mobile in 1701. Expansion threatened the Spanish position both in Florida and in Texas. In 1719 the French captured Pensacola, the major Spanish base in west Florida, in a surprise attack, but it was recaptured by an expedition of 1,400 troops from Havana, and was then retaken by the French and their local allies, the Choctaws. Pensacola was returned to the Spaniards when the two sides made peace. The

Cape Town. A Dutch base established in 1652, this was an important position on the route to India as well as the base for expansion into the interior. The arrival of a French fleet thwarted a British attempt to capture Cape Town during the War of American Independence, but it was taken in 1795. Such positions were very vulnerable to amphibious attack.

The British capture of Havana, 1762. This successful attack wrecked Spanish naval power in the West Indies, and the Spaniards had to cede Florida at the subsequent peace to regain Cuba. However, heavy losses to malaria and yellow fever during the siege destroyed much of the army that had been brought to a high pitch of combat readiness during the conquest of Canada, weakening the British military response to the American revolution in 1775.

Spaniards sent a force from Santa Fé in 1720 to counter the French expansion, but most of it was wiped out by natives on the South Platte. Another large force was sent across Texas in 1721; nevertheless, this war was swiftly brought to an end. The rivalry between these two colonial powers was generally peaceful.

In general, the Spanish empire was less often a target for British attack than its ally, France. Spanish America was less vulnerable to attack, largely because it was far more populous and much less dependent for defence and finances on trade with the homeland. Tropical disease also made attack on the Spanish empire hazardous: Havana fell to the British in 1762, but they lost about 6,000 men, largely to yellow fever and malaria. In 1780 the British lost 77 per cent of their force, most of them to disease, when they attacked the Spaniards in modern Nicaragua, and the operation was then abandoned. The Spaniards, in turn, sought to expel British traders from their positions on the Caribbean coast of Central America (on the Mosquito Coast of modern Nicaragua and what is now Belize). The port of Belize itself was briefly captured in 1754. However, neither power devoted more than desultory interest to this issue.

The major colonial conflicts were between Britain and France. As with other overseas struggles between European powers, this conflict interacted with those between native polities and between these polities and the Europeans. This interaction caused a diffusion of weaponry and military techniques from the Europeans to others. This was particularly apparent in India, where both Britain and France provided military assistance to their allies, but it was also important elsewhere. Thus, when in 1779 Lord North, the British Prime Minister, was faced with Spain's entry into the War of American Independence on the side of France and the Americans, he suggested that 'if a little money or arms or the assistance of an engineer could stir up the Algerines or Moors to make war against the Spaniards and to attack their garrisons in Africa, I should think it worth while to make the attempt, as such a diversion of the Spanish force would be of no inconsiderable service to us'. Over the following decade, the French provided engineers to help improve Turkish fortifications against the Russians for similar reasons.

With the benefit of hindsight, the course of the Anglo-French conflict appears all too clear: France would be on the defensive, increasingly pressed by a power that was stronger at sea and thus able to take the initiative; with the support of their North American colonies, which were far more heavily populated than their French counterparts, the British were bound to win there.

However, the situation was far more complex than that. It was not in fact inevitable that the British would win and not obvious that they would dominate the oceans or take the initiative, or that if they did take it that they would necessarily be successful. Thus, attempts on Québec in 1690 and 1711 failed. In the latter case, nine ships were wrecked in fogs and gales in the poorly charted St Lawrence and the badly managed expedition turned back.

In the War of the Austrian Succession, France took the initiative in India, taking Madras in 1746 and then, in 1748, holding off a British offensive against their base, Pondicherry. The British captured the major base of Louisbourg on Cape Breton Island in 1745, but in the following year the French were able to send a large expedition to North American waters, although, owing to disease, storms and an absence of local bases and supplies, it failed to retake Louisbourg. The fleet returned to France with the loss of 8,000 men. The fortress itself had cost 1–2 per cent of the annual budget of the French Ministry of the Marine between 1716 and 1740.

The Seven Years War (1756–63), known in America as the French and Indian War (1754–63), is generally seen as a period of British success, spectacularly so in 1759, the 'Year of Victories', when the British captured Québec and Guadeloupe and defeated the French fleet in European waters at Lagos and Quiberon Bay. A second year of victories in 1762 saw Martinique taken from the French and Havana and Manila from their Spanish allies. Other British successes in that war included, in 1758, the capture of Forts Louis and Gorée, the French bases in west Africa, as well as Louisbourg; in 1760, the surrender of Montréal and the French army in Canada, as well as Eyre Coote's defeat of the French army in India under Thomas-Arthur de Baron de Lally Tallendal at Wandewash (22 January); in 1761,

On the last night of the 1758 siege of Louisbourg, British warships penetrated the harbour and destroyed the two remaining French warships. The besieging force was stronger than in 1745, but again army–navy co-operation was crucial and the landward defences were breached by British cannon. Québec the following year was a more formidable challenge, as the British amphibious force could not cut it off from its hinterland.

Sir Hector Munro's capture of the major French base in India at Pondicherry in 1778 owed much to support from Sir Edward Vernon's blockading squadron. Vernon landed marines and sailors to help Munro, who bombarded the city with twenty-eight heavy cannon and twenty-seven mortars. The attack in 1748 had been unsuccessful, but Pondicherry also fell in 1761 and 1793.

the capture of the last, and most important, French base in India, Pondicherry.

These triumphs reflected the ability to combine local and distant resources. Thus, North American militia, Native American allies and Indian sepoys all contributed manpower, and food and transport (mules, bullocks, oxen, wagons) were acquired locally. However, it was also necessary to bring troops and munitions, especially cannon, on long, hazardous and unpredictable journeys from Britain. The ability to do so was crucial to British military capability, and was enhanced by the establishment of storage points, garrisons from which troops and munitions could be obtained. Both improved the confidence of British military planning. The operation of the system can be seen in the expedition against Spanish-held Cartagena in modern Colombia in 1741. The British force included not only troops from Britain, but also men raised in Jamaica and Britain's North American colonies.

However, the Cartagena expedition was a disaster. The strength of the Spanish defences and a failure of army–navy co-operation were serious blows, but it was yellow fever that really defeated the British. Over 10,000 troops died on the expedition, most from disease: long sieges in the tropics were fatal.

There were also serious British failures during the Seven Years War, including

Elephant armour. Elephants had played a major military role in India in the sixteenth and seventeenth centuries, and were effective against massed infantry, but were vulnerable to mounted archers and firearms, and by the eighteenth century were generally deployed mainly for effect. To Europeans, they symbolized the exotic in Asian warfare. Elephants remained more important in south-east Asia.

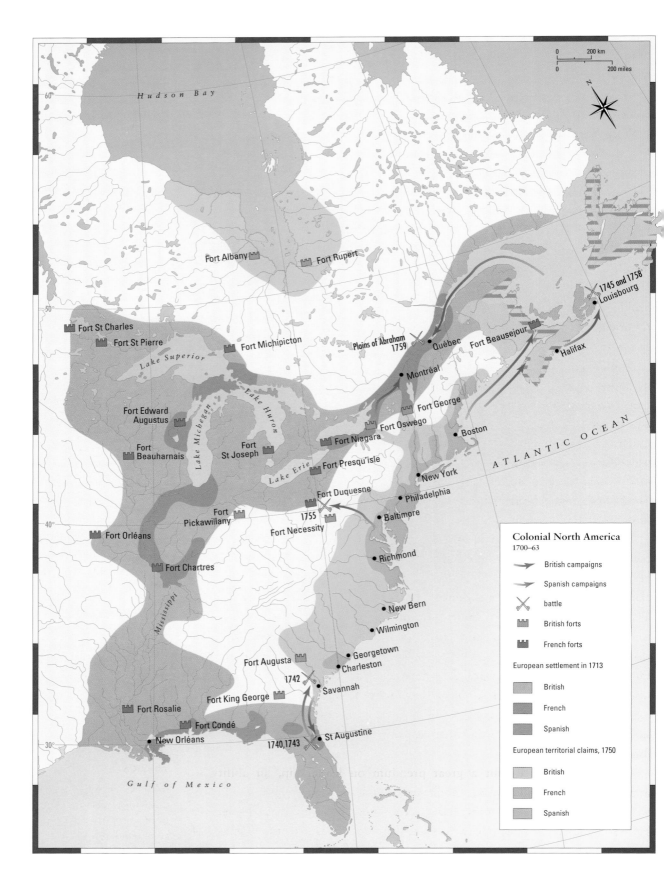

0   200 km

0   200 miles

N

H u d s o n   B a y

60°

Fort Albany

Fort Rupert

1745 and 1758
Louisbourg

50°

Fort St Charles

Fort St Pierre

Fort Michipicton

Plains of Abraham
1759

Québec

Fort Beausejour

Halifax

Lake Superior

Montréal

Lake Michigan

Lake Huron

Fort Edward
Augustus

Fort George

Fort Oswego

Boston

Fort
Beauharnais

Fort
St Joseph

Fort Niagara

Lake Erie

Fort Presqu'isle

New York

Fort Duquesne

Philadelphia

Fort
Pickawillany

1755

Baltimore

40°

Fort Orléans

Fort Necessity

Fort Chartres

Richmond

Mississippi

New Bern

Wilmington

Fort Augusta

Georgetown

Charleston

1742

Savannah

Fort King George

Fort Rosalie

Fort Condé

New Orléans

1740, 1743

St Augustine

30°

Gulf of Mexico

A T L A N T I C   O C E A N

Colonial North America
1700–63

⟶ British campaigns

⟶ Spanish campaigns

✕ battle

🏰 British forts

🏰 French forts

European settlement in 1713

British

French

Spanish

European territorial claims, 1750

British

French

Spanish

the successful French–native ambush of General Braddock's larger army at the battle of Monongahela on 9 July 1755, the loss of Forts Ontario, George, Oswego and William Henry to French advances in North America in 1756 and 1757, the abortive plan to capture Louisbourg in 1757, the heavy losses in the badly managed and unsuccessful frontal attack on Carillon (Ticonderoga) in 1758, the defeat of the army outside Québec in April 1760 (the battle of Sainte-Foy), and, in India, the loss of Fort St David in 1758. These British failures serve as a reminder of the difficulty of the task, not least because of the complications of amphibious operations, the problems of operating in the interior of North America, the need to allocate limited resources across a number of spheres and the resourcefulness of some French commanders, especially Lally in India and Montcalm in Canada. Indeed, even successes were often obtained only after considerable difficulties. Thus, the capture of Québec followed a frustrating two months in which the natural strength of the position, French fortifications and the skilful character of Montcalm's dispositions had thwarted the British force under James Wolfe.

Battle of Monongahela, 9 July 1755. The response by the larger but untrained British force to the French–native ambush was inadequate. Instead of attacking, they held their ground, thus offering excellent targets. A total of 977 of the 1,459 British troops were killed or wounded.

The close similarity of weaponry and methods of fighting between the combatants ensured that these battles were different to, for example, those between the British and Indians. The French defeat outside Québec in 1759, for example, was similar to an engagement between the British and French in Europe. The major difference was the size of the armies. Wolfe climbed the riverside cliffs to the Plains of Abraham outside Québec with fewer than 4,500 men, while the casualties on 13 September were about 650 on each side. Decisive battles in Europe involved much larger forces, for example 89,000 men in total at Leuthen in 1757 and 62,000 at Rossbach in the same year. A large British army was sent against Havana in 1762, but only 1,738 men were dispatched against Manila the same year, and that figure included French deserters and 100 lascars as a labour force.

These small forces put a great premium on leadership, an ability to understand and exploit terrain, morale, unit cohesion and fire-power. The British were generally adept at all of these, but so too were their opponents – sometimes more so. Thus, in 1757 Montcalm's understanding of warfare in the interior of North America, combined with his effective use of French troops and native

COLONIAL NORTH AMERICA

Relatively small European forces fought over vast distances thanks in part to native allies. British victory was far from inevitable.

THE FALL OF FRENCH CANADA

'With a vast land and sea force in North America, nothing has been done.' The complaint in the Herald of 20 October 1757 could not be repeated. Within three years, Canada had been conquered.

allies, enabled him to capture Fort William Henry. Nevertheless, outside Québec on 13 September 1759 it was British fire-power that was superior. A British general volley settled the battle, halting the advancing French columns. A second volley was the prelude to a successful bayonet charge. French morale was shattered. Although Québec had not been captured and more French troops arrived immediately after the battle, the French officers decided at a council of war not to risk battle again, but to retreat up-river. The decision was subsequently reversed, but, even as a French relief force was approaching Québec, it surrendered on 18 September 1759.

The duration of the struggle was also significant: had the war ended in 1758,

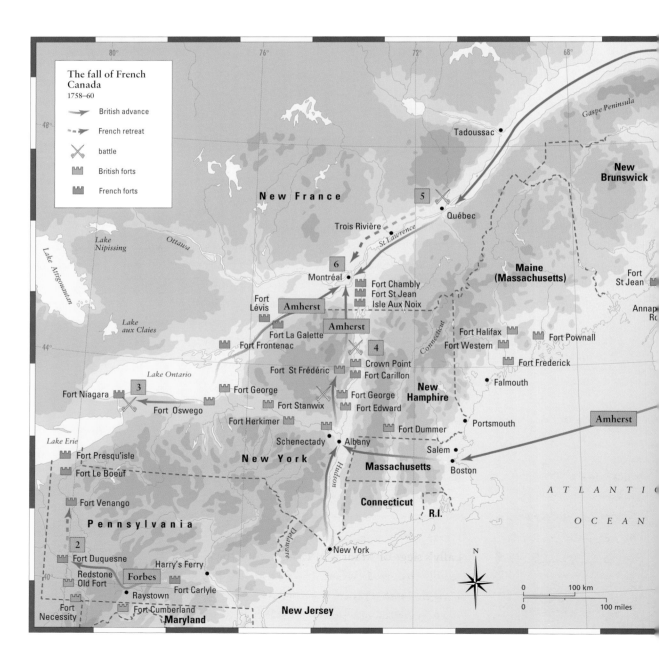

or even at the end of April 1760, it would not have been anywhere near as successful for the British. Furthermore, the interconnected nature of the war could be as important as conflicts in particular areas. The French were resilient in Canada, but the British sent very many more troops there than their opponents, and, at the crisis of the war, in 1760, when the French besieged Québec after their victory at the battle of Sainte-Foy, the garrison was relieved when a British fleet arrived with reinforcements and the French were forced back to Montréal. The British also benefited from their ability to learn how to operate most effectively in North America: light infantry units were developed, the importance of woodcraft was appreciated and logistics in the vast interior of North America improved.

Naval predominance and success in European waters meant an ability to grasp the initiative outside Europe. That was the vital interconnectedness of British power. It is claimed sometimes that the British conquered America in Germany; meaning that the concentration of French troops in Germany during the Seven Years War deprived Montcalm of men. Certainly this concentration caused him to take a defensive position in 1758–9 and to abandon his earlier advance towards the Hudson Valley. But it would be more appropriate to argue that the British conquered Canada off Brest: that the blockade of the leading French naval port, a blockade that led ultimately to the victory at Quiberon Bay in 1759, made it impossible for France to retain the initiative in North America or indeed to send substantial reinforcements to their colonies there or maintain important trade links with them. The French imperial system had collapsed before the British captured the French colonies. The control and organization of maritime links was vital, because of demographic, organizational, economic, and, more narrowly, military factors. With no large hinterland, the French colonies were vulnerable to amphibious attack; British naval strength, on the other hand, meant that French attacks on British positions, such as Lally's siege of Madras in 1758–9, could be more readily thwarted. Whereas in Europe the British struggle with France was that of a maritime versus a continental power, outside Europe it was a between two maritime powers.

OVERLEAF: *A British participant in Wolfe's victory over the French outside Québec on 13 September 1759 recorded, 'About 9 o'clock the French army had drawn up under the walls of the town, and advanced towards us briskly and in good order. We stood to receive them; they began their fire at a distance, we reserved ours, and as they came nearer fired on them by divisions, this did execution and seemed to check them a little, however they still advanced pretty quick, we increased our fire without altering our position, and, when they were within less than an hundred yards, gave them a full fire, fixed our bayonets, and under cover of the smoke the whole line charged.'*

Anticosti Island

Wolfe

Isle Madeleine

Cape Breton Island

Isle St Jean

Louisbourg

Fort Cumberland
Fort Lawrence

[1]

Scotia

Amherst

Halifax

British Victories

1	Louisbourg, 26 July 1758
2	Fort Duquesne, November 1758
3	La Belle-Famille, 24 July 1759
4	Crown Point, 31 July 1759
5	Québec, 18 September 1759
6	Montréal, Governor Vaudreuil surrenders, 8 September 1760

CHAPTER FOUR

The American War of Independence

George Washington. *Although tactically maladroit, most obviously at Long Island and Brandywine, Washington learned from his mistakes and was also a very effective political general. His ambition, however, was at the service of the revolution: Washington was no Napoleon.*

THE AMERICAN WAR OF INDEPENDENCE

THE RELATIVE SITUATION of Britain and France was very different during the American War of Independence (1775–83): first, the British were up against a continental opponent, the American revolutionaries, and, second, they lost their naval dominance in the related struggle with France (1778–83), a struggle that broadened out as the Spanish and the Dutch entered the war on the French side in 1779 and 1780 respectively.

The American war was the first example of a transoceanic conflict fought between a European colonial power and subjects of European descent, and the first example of a major revolutionary war, a struggle for independence in which the notion of the citizenry under arms played a crucial role. The creation of the new state was accompanied by the creation of a new type of army; both reflected a more dynamic and egalitarian society than that of Europe (but not for the sixth of the population who were slaves). Although many of the commanders of the revolutionary force, the Continental Army, were from the wealthier section of society, the social range of the American leadership was far greater than that in European armies and discipline was different. This was not an army of serfs but of citizens. The degree to which the army represented a new political identity and social practice helped to sustain its cohesion and even the continuation of the revolutionary cause when the war went badly, as in the winter of 1777–8, when the army camped at Valley Forge after the loss of the capital, Philadelphia.

However, it would be misleading to exaggerate the novelty of the war in terms of battlefield operations. It was essentially fought on terms that would have been familiar to those who had been engaged in the Seven Years War. The American response to battle was to adopt the line formations of musketeers of European warfare. This course was advocated by George Washington (1732–99), the commander of the Continental Army, who had served in the Virginia forces in the Seven Years War, taking part in advances against the French in 1754, 1755 and 1758. Washington was

Battle of Lexington, 19 April 1775. The first clash of the Revolution when British infantry, en route to seize arms at Concord, scattered outnumbered colonial militia. Brigadier General Hugh Percy wrote of the British withdrawal: 'there was not a stone wall, or house ... from whence the rebels did not fire upon us'. The shedding of American blood outraged New England.

a believer in position warfare, although he was also willing to use the militia as partisans.

The alternative strategy, advocated by Major General Charles Lee (1731–82), which centred on irregular warfare, especially the avoidance of position warfare and battle, was not followed up, except in 1781 after defeats in the south. The British would have found it difficult to identify targets had such a strategy been followed. Lee himself was a former British regular officer who had served in North America (1755–60) and Portugal (1762), before serving in the Polish army, which had to contend with the greater strength of Russia.

Both the Americans and the British fought in a more open order with more significant gaps between the units than was the norm in Europe, because the

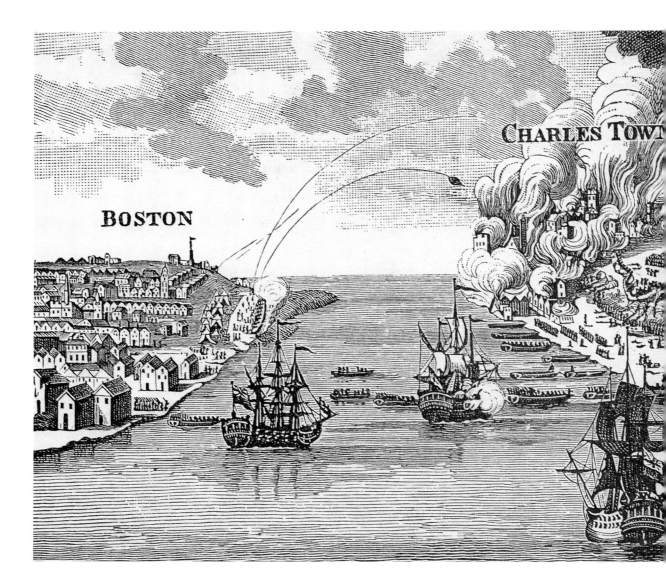

BOSTON

CHARLES TOW

The British General John Burgoyne recorded 'one of the greatest scenes of war that can be conceived ... Howe's corps ascending the hill in the face of entrenchments and a very disadvantageous ground warmly engaged to the left of the enemy ... and in the arm of the sea, our ships and floating batteries cannonading them.'

general absence of cavalry made the infantry less vulnerable to attack, while the enclosed nature of much of the terrain encouraged deployments that reflected the topography. Artillery and fortifications also played a smaller role than in conflict in western Europe – for example in the British campaigns in Westphalia and Hesse in 1758–62 – while, as more generally with transoceanic operations, the force–distance relationship was different: here relatively small armies operated across great distances in a war in which there were no real fronts.

Although the British had extensive earlier experience of campaigning against the French in North America, American tactics were still able to pose major problems for them, especially when the Americans took advantage of the terrain. In 1775, Alexander Campbell complained of the Americans from Boston that 'they are a cowardly set that will not fight but when fenced by trees, houses or trenches'. At the battle of Long Island (27 August 1776), Captain William Congreve of the British artillery recorded:

BATTLE OF BUNKER HILL, 17 JUNE 1775

The British moved ponderously, advancing in traditional open field formation on the American entrenchments. The British artillery failed to damage the American position, and the Americans shattered the first two attacks with heavy musket fire, before running short of ammunition and being pushed back by the third attack. The British were to fight better in subsequent battles, but their failure at Bunker Hill was crucial.

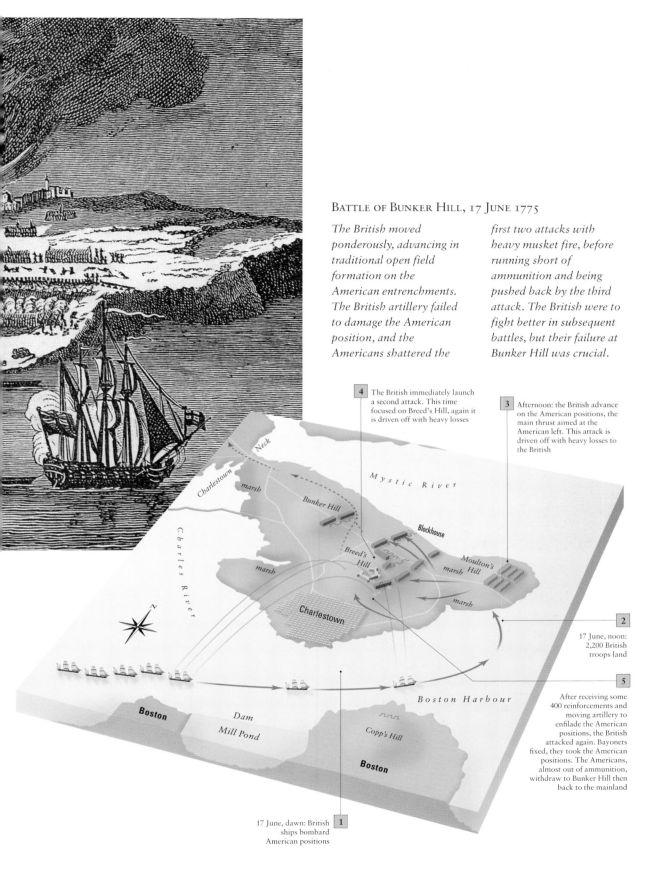

4 The British immediately launch a second attack. This time focused on Breed's Hill, again it is driven off with heavy losses

3 Afternoon: the British advance on the American positions, the main thrust aimed at the American left. This attack is driven off with heavy losses to the British

2 17 June, noon: 2,200 British troops land

5 After receiving some 400 reinforcements and moving artillery to enfilade the American positions, the British attacked again. Bayonets fixed, they took the American positions. The Americans, almost out of ammunition, withdraw to Bunker Hill then back to the mainland

1 17 June, dawn: British ships bombard American positions

Neck
Charlestown
marsh
Bunker Hill
Mystic River
Blockhouse
Breed's Hill
Moulton's Hill
marsh
Charles River
marsh
marsh
Charlestown
N
Boston Harbour
Boston
Dam
Mill Pond
Copp's Hill
Boston

Four different uniforms worn by the revolutionary soldiers, by Jean-Baptiste-Antoine de Verger, a French observer. The provision of uniforms was an important aspect of the regularization of the revolutionary military effort. The existence of units from different states, and of the militia alongside the Continental Army, complicated the military structure.

THE AMERICAN WAR OF INDEPENDENCE

Britain was defeated but, from 1778, when confronted by a powerful European–American coalition, showed impressive resilience. The war revealed the problems posed by the absence of a large army. The British forces operating in the field were often quite small in number.

BATTLES

Map 1

1 Lexington, 19 April 1775

2 Bunker Hill, 17 June 1775

Map 2

1 Princeton, 3 January 1777

2 Oriskany, 6 August 1777

3 Bennington, 15 August 1777

4 Brandywine, 11 September 1777

5 Freeman's farm, 19 September 1777

6 Paoli, 20 September 1777

7 Bemis Heights, 7 October 1777

8 Germantown, 4 October 1777

Map 3

1 Monmouth Court House, 28 June 1778

2 Savannah, 29 December 1778

3 Augusta, 29 January 1779

4 Briar Creek, 3 March 1779

5 Camden, 16 August 1780

6 King's Mountain, 7 October 1780

7 Blackstock, 20 November 1780

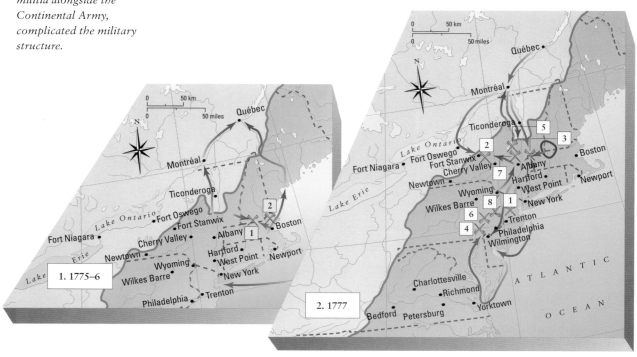

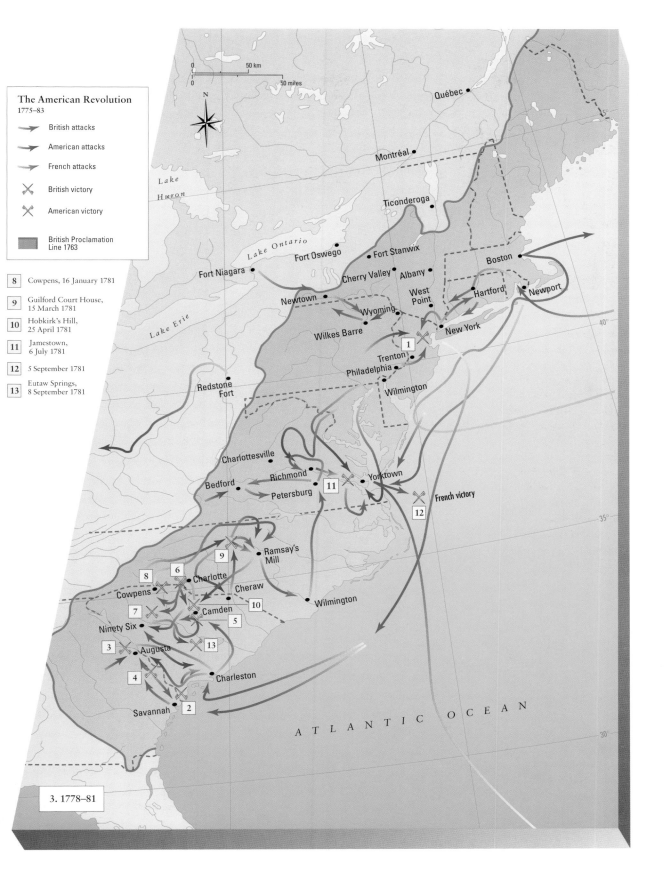

The American Revolution
1775–83

→ British attacks

→ American attacks

→ French attacks

✕ British victory

✕ American victory

British Proclamation
Line 1763

8 Cowpens, 16 January 1781

9 Guilford Court House,
15 March 1781

10 Hobkirk's Hill,
25 April 1781

11 Jamestown,
6 July 1781

12 5 September 1781

13 Eutaw Springs,
8 September 1781

Québec

Montréal

Ticonderoga

Lake
Huron

Lake Ontario

Fort Oswego

Fort Stanwix

Boston

Fort Niagara

Cherry Valley

Albany

Newport

Newtown

West
Point

Hartford

Lake Erie

Wyoming

New York

Wilkes Barre

1

Redstone
Fort

Trenton

Philadelphia

Wilmington

Charlottesville

Richmond

Yorktown

Bedford

11

Petersburg

12 French victory

Ramsay's
Mill

9

8

6

Charlotte

Cheraw

Cowpens

10

7

Camden

Wilmington

Ninety Six

5

3

Augusta

13

4

Charleston

Savannah

2

ATLANTIC OCEAN

3. 1778–81

I found the enemy numerous and supported by the 6-pounders [cannon]. However, by plying them smartly with grapeshot their guns were soon drawn off but the riflemen being covered by trees and large stones had very much the advantage of us, who were upon the open ground ... [had] not the light infantry of the Guards ... come up in time I believe we should all have been cut off.

In positional warfare the Americans could be defeated, their troops outflanked, as at Long Island and Brandywine (11 September 1777), or their strongholds captured, as at Fort Washington (1776) and Charleston (1780); but the more mobile American units could operate with deadly effect.

The major role of the American militia created a problem, both in operational terms, for example by restricting the range of the British supply gatherers, and in the political context of the conflict, especially in harrying Loyalists, the large number of Americans who supported continued allegiance to the British crown. The militia helped to ensure that the British were outnumbered and thus limited their effectiveness as an occupation force.

American fighting techniques could also be a problem for the British on the battleground. At Bemis Heights, in September 1777, their riflemen, under Daniel Morgan, concentrated on picking off British officers. The defeated British commander, General John Burgoyne, wrote subsequently:

The enemy had with their army great numbers of marksmen, armed with rifle-barrel pieces: these, during an engagement, hovered upon the flanks in small detachments, and were very expert in securing themselves and in shifting their ground. In this action, many placed themselves in high trees in the rear of their own line, and there was seldom a minute's interval of smoke in any part of our line without officers being taken off by single shots.

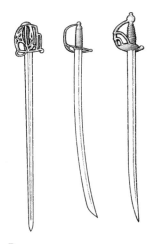

BRITISH CAVALRY AND INFANTRY SWORDS

LEFT: *cavalry sword, c. 1770;* CENTRE: *infantry officer's sword, 1786 pattern, a type generally known as a spadroon;* RIGHT: *infantry hanger, 1751 pattern sword. Swords continued to play a major role in European cavalry combat but were only used by officers in infantry conflict.*

It is only too easy to assume that the war was a foregone conclusion, that the British could not conquer the Thirteen Colonies and that their defeat was inevitable because they employed an anachronistic method of warfare. This is questionable, however, and any reading of the correspondence of American generals underlines the difficulties of their task. Colonel James Clinton wrote to Washington from Fort Constitution, a crucial position in the Hudson Valley, in July 1776, 'We want more officers of the artillery here very much ... we are scarce of gun flints and good arms.' Captain Richard Varick wrote from Albany, 'No copper, lead or tin is to be had between this place and New York.' The following month, Washington wrote from New York that his army was 'weak' and heavily outnumbered and, in another letter, 'I cannot help feeling very anxious apprehensions. The new levies are so incomplete, the old regiments deficient in their compliment.'

On 16 September 1776 Washington reported on the British landing at Kip's Bay on the east side of Manhattan Island, the previous day:

I found the troops that had been posted in the lines retreating with the utmost precipitation and those ordered to support them ... flying in every direction and in the greatest confusion, notwithstanding the exertions of their generals to form them. I used every means in my power to rally and get them into some order but my attempts were fruitless and ineffectual.

In October he wrote, 'We want both flour and beef ... the fatal consequences attendant on mutiny and plunder must ensue'. The British, of course, also faced serious problems, particularly with logistics, but Washington's correspondence shows that there was no major capability gap in favour of the revolutionaries. By the time of French entry into the war in 1778, the Americans had forced the British out of New England (March 1776), repulsed the advance on Philadelphia from the north-east at Trenton (26 December 1776), challenged the British capture of Philadelphia by mounting a riposte at Germantown (4 October 1777), and defeated Burgoyne's advance south from Canada (Saratoga capitulation,

British surrender at Saratoga, 17 October 1777. Pushing south from Canada into the Hudson valley, General Burgoyne's army was dangerously exposed to larger American forces and unable to break through their positions at Bemis Heights. Saratoga ended any serious prospect of cutting off New England from the rest of America.

THE WAR NEARLY WON

The British came closest to victory in their 1776 campaign, but Washington's victory at Trenton stemmed their tide.

The landing of British troops in New York, 1776. Having defeated the Americans on Long Island, the British used the navy to mount outflanking amphibious operations on Manhattan Island, thanks to which the outnumbered Americans were driven from New York. It remained the major British base for the rest of the war and, even after his victory at Yorktown, Washington was not strong enough to capture the city.

17 October 1777). Yet they had also failed to sustain their own invasion of Canada (1775–6), retreating to Crown Point after a defeat at Three Rivers (8 June 1776), and they lost New York (1776), Newport (1776) and Philadelphia (1777).

The Americans probably benefited in the long run from being driven out of Canada. Such extended lines of communication and supply, and the commitment of manpower required, would have bled their army dry and possibly led to mutinies. Washington reflected on the failure to take Québec, relieved by the British on 6 May 1776, 'hence I shall know the events of war are exceedingly doubtful, and that capricious fortune often blasts our most flattering hopes'. Without Canada, the Americans maintained their advantage of interior lines. This was important in responding to the British offensives in 1776 and 1777. The fall of New York was a major blow, but the initiative was regained by Washington's success at Trenton. During the subsequent war of attrition in New Jersey in January–May 1777, the frequent and devastating attacks by American forces on British outposts and foraging parties demonstrated their capability. Washington's increasing employment of light infantry enhanced American strength, as did the British delay in mobilizing the Loyalists.

French intervention altered the situation, by adding to the range of urgent British military commitments elsewhere in the world, thus diverting British resources; first, by threatening British naval control of North American waters and thereby challenging the application of these resources and the articulation

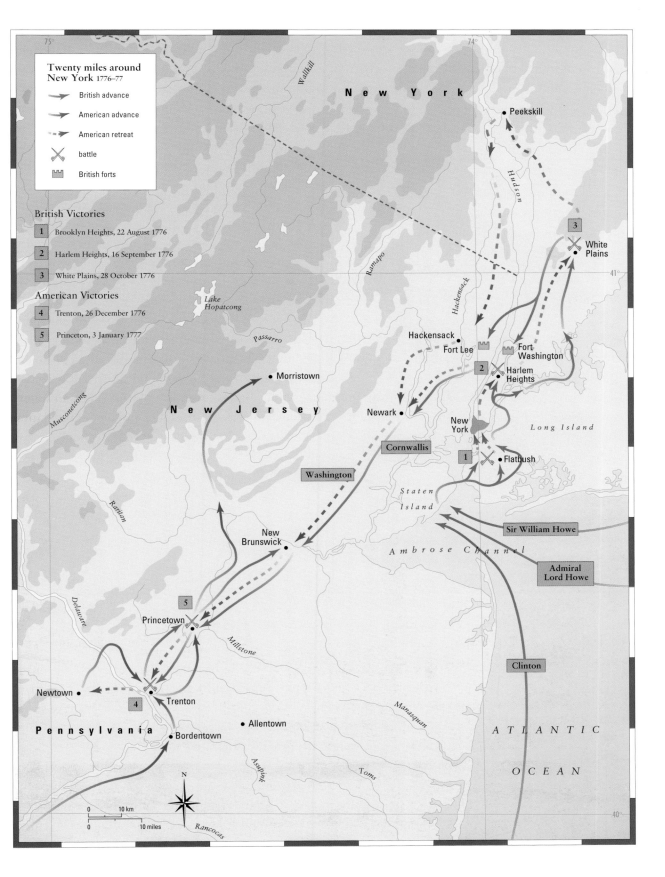

Twenty miles around New York 1776–77

→ British advance

→ American advance

⇢ American retreat

✕ battle

🏰 British forts

British Victories

1 Brooklyn Heights, 22 August 1776

2 Harlem Heights, 16 September 1776

3 White Plains, 28 October 1776

American Victories

4 Trenton, 26 December 1776

5 Princeton, 3 January 1777

New York

Peekskill

Wallkill

Hudson

3 White Plains

Ramapo

Hackensack

Hackensack
Fort Lee

Fort Washington

2 Harlem Heights

Passarro

Lake Hopatcong

Morristown

New Jersey

Newark

New York

Long Island

Cornwallis

1

Flatbush

Staten Island

Washington

Musconetcong

Raritan

New Brunswick

Ambrose Channel

Sir William Howe

Admiral Lord Howe

Delaware

5

Princetown

Millstone

Clinton

Newtown

4

Trenton

Manasquan

Pennsylvania

Allentown

Bordentown

Assipink

Toms

ATLANTIC

OCEAN

N

0   10 km

0   10 miles

Rancocas

of the British imperial system; and second, by sending an expeditionary force under Count Jean de Rochambeau, a veteran of French campaigns in Germany in the War of the Austrian Succession and the Seven Years War, to North America in 1780, and thus ensuring that the French threat there was not only a naval one. Another aspect of the same process was offered by the Spanish conquest of west Florida, that began when Spain entered the war in 1779, taking Baton Rouge, Manchac and Natchez, and that culminated with the capture of Pensacola in 1781: a Spanish grenade ignited a gunpowder magazine, leading to the overthrow of the defences.

The more serious nature of the military challenge once France and Spain had entered the war increased the pressure on British political and military leaders, but they had no additional resources. Furthermore, the customary problems of poor communications in the age of sail, and the consequences both for command and control and for transport and supply, were accentuated by the scale of the war and the interconnections between different spheres, most obviously naval operations in the Caribbean and off North America.

French intervention did not automatically lead to British defeats. Indeed, Franco-American attacks on British positions at Newport (1778) and Savannah (1779) were unsuccessful. Nevertheless, British moves had now to be made against the background of a possible French response. This led the British to abandon Philadelphia (1778), and to concentrate on the southern colonies. There, they succeeded in capturing Savannah (December 1778)

General Horatio Gates (1725–1806). Born in England and a veteran of the Seven Years War (wounded in Braddock's defeat and took part in capture of Martinique), Gates settled in Virginia, and was appointed Adjutant General of the Continental Army in 1775. Successful at Saratoga in 1777, he was defeated at Camden on 16 August 1780 and replaced.

and Charleston (May 1780), but found it difficult to consolidate their position in South Carolina. Victories – over Horatio Gates at Camden (16 August 1780) and, less easily, over Nathanael Greene at Guildford Court House (15 March 1781) – did not bring permanent control; on the contrary, a partisan war broke out over much of the south.

The British commander, Lord Cornwallis, pressed north into Virginia, in the hope that he could thereby improve the situation. Once there, however, he failed to crush American resistance and soon surrendered the initiative, establishing himself at Yorktown, a poor defensive position; however, it had an anchorage suitable for ships of the line, so that he would be able to withdraw if necessary. At this point, the war in America was far from over, although it was apparent that neither the southern strategy nor the advance into Virginia had brought

Nathanael Greene (1742–86). One of the more effective American generals, Greene was an effective administrator and good strategist. Succeeded Gates as commander in the south, he made Cornwallis's victory at Guilford Courthouse on 15 March 1781 hard won. Thereafter, Greene's operations helped restrict the British to the environs of Charleston and Savannah.

the anticipated gains. Nevertheless, as earlier around New York, the British had shown that they could gain and hold important points and defeat American field forces.

However, at this juncture, the movement from the West Indies of the French fleet under Count François de Grasse denied the British command of the sea. Furthermore, Washington and Rochambeau were able to achieve a concentration of strength on land outside Yorktown which placed Cornwallis in an untenable position. The failure of Admiral Graves to defeat the French off the Virginia Capes and force his way into the Chesapeake on 5 September 1781 was indecisive in terms of casualties, but, as it prevented the relief of Cornwallis, it was an important success for the French.

Blockaded, under heavy bombardment and without relief, Cornwallis

WARFARE IN THE EIGHTEENTH CENTURY

Surrender of British under Cornwallis at Yorktown, 19 October 1781. The consequence of the static defence of an exposed coastal position without naval support. Without the French fleet at the mouth of the Chesapeake, Cornwallis would have been able to extricate his force.

surrendered on 19 October 1781. Two days earlier, Johann Conrad Döhla, a member of the Ansbach-Bayreuth forces in Cornwallis's army, recorded:

> At daybreak the enemy bombardment resumed, more terribly strong than ever before. They fired from all positions without let-up. Our command, which was in the Hornwork, could hardly tolerate the enemy bombs, howitzer, and cannonballs any longer. There was nothing to be seen but bombs and cannonballs raining down on our entire line.

Although the British still held Charleston, New York and Savannah, this was effectively the end of the war in North America. News of the defeat led to the replacement of Lord North's ministry by a British government more ready to accept American independence. Thereafter, although American advances on British bases were held off, the British concentrated on their conflict with the Bourbons (France and Spain) and, in the eventual peace treaty, the Treaty of

Versailles of 1783, the British agreed to surrender New York, Charleston and Savannah, as well as the 'Old North-west', the territory between the Appalachians and the Great Lakes.

In some respects, the war with the Bourbons was similar to the fighting in North America: the British did badly, but avoided complete collapse, and the progress of the war on land depended in large part on naval operations. Many other generals could have written as did Sir John Burgoyne from Madras in 1782, 'it is by the sea only we can be supplied'. This was true of India, Sri Lanka, the West Indies, west Florida, Gibraltar and Cape Town. British initiatives, such as the plan to capture Cape Town from the Dutch in 1781, were thwarted by the arrival of French warships. Likewise, besieged British positions, such as Québec in 1776 and Gibraltar from 1779, were relieved by the British fleet, while those that were not relieved, such as Pensacola in west Florida and Menorca in the Mediterranean, were lost in 1781 and 1782 respectively.

Nevertheless, the British were helped by the failure of the most important

Siege of Gibraltar, 1782. The long siege of 1779–83 was thwarted by the strength of the defence and three successful reliefs by sea. This contrasted with the fate of Cornwallis's army at Yorktown. The British had seized Gibraltar in 1704.

Bourbon naval schemes – the attempted invasion of southern England in 1779, and the deployment of a large fleet in the Caribbean in 1782, which, it was feared, might attack Jamaica. Furthermore, although they were hard pressed in southern India by the French and their ally Mysore, the British situation there did not collapse on either land or sea, partly because, in a major deployment of transoceanic strength, ten regiments reached India in 1780–82. Furthermore, the British fleet in Indian waters under Rear Admiral Sir Edward Hughes displayed great resilience.

The avoidance of disaster is scarcely heroic, but, given the strength of the respective sides, this was a major achievement for Britain. Without assured naval dominance, the articulation of the British military system was weak and the success of the individual parts limited, but the loss of British dominance did not mean that the Bourbons had gained it; although the Americans had effective privateers, their weak continental navy was able to provide no assistance to the Bourbons.

The war was messy, in large part because neither side was able to predict the likely success of their initiatives. This was a particular problem for states attempting to plan operations on a transoceanic, if not global, scale. However, it is remarkable that states such as Britain and France could mount the logistical effort required to deploy considerable forces at such great distances. They could survive defeat, and return to the attack, proceeding systematically to a planned military outcome. The growing role of the state in European warfare, replacing the semi-independent military entrepreneurs of earlier days, was readily apparent, not least in terms of a higher level of military preparedness and planning. In 1787 Henry Dundas, who controlled the Indian policy of the British government, wrote to Cornwallis, then governor-general and commander-in-chief in India:

> I have made up my mind to it as a principle of Indian administration, that we ought at all times to keep a force there not only for defence, but for active operations. When the occasion occurs, it will be too late to be recruiting your European army in India, or to be increasing it from a peace to a war establishment. It must be at all times kept on such a scale, as that upon the receipt of a letter from this country, your Lordship or any other person in the administration of India, must be instantly ready to begin offensive operations against Pondicherry, Trincomali, the Dutch possessions in the Eastern Isles [Java, Sumatra]; or, in short, anywhere.

Centrally directed resources and power applied at long range: neither was new, but the increasing scale of both – demonstrated most obviously by European transoceanic states, most clearly in the Seven Years War and the War of American Independence – makes it unhelpful to stress the limitations and indecisiveness of warfare in this period. This was even true of relatively weak states. The Dutch government appreciated that their colonial empire in the east had become vulnerable to Britain, which now had the capability to invade the East Indies despite the great distance from Europe. As a result, the Dutch government, for the first time, sent a naval squadron to the East Indies, as the armed forces provided by the now almost bankrupt Dutch East India Company were insufficient to defend their positions.

Britain and her former American colonies did not fight again until the war of 1812. This struggle, waged from 1812 to 1815 (although peace was negotiated in late 1814), was very different to the earlier conflict and, as was so often the case, the difference was primarily a matter of political context. From the outset, the war was secondary to the British struggle against France, and it was only when Napoleon abdicated in 1814 that large British forces could be sent to North America, the forces that made possible operations in the Chesapeake, including the temporary occupation of Washington in 1814, as well as the disastrous advance on New Orleans early in 1815, a head-on assault on well-entrenched American troops commanded by Andrew Jackson which was bloodily repelled on 8 January. Although there was much opposition to the war within the USA, there was no civil war there. The British forces were a foreign force, attackers, not participants in a revolutionary struggle within the Thirteen Colonies.

The war itself forms an interesting contrast to the French Revolutionary and Napoleonic struggle. Whereas France's military system had been energized and tempered by long years of struggle, the American forces had suffered from years of neglect after the War of Independence, from unrealistic political expectations and poor direction. This led to failure in the early stages of the conflict, when Britain was weak, and the Americans attacked Canada in 1812 and 1813, and again in 1814, when the British campaigned on the shores of the Chesapeake. In short, the Americans had a weak army and an unhelpful political structure; both a contrast to the situation in France, and, indeed, in Britain in the early 1810s. Had the British devoted resources comparable to those employed against Napoleon then they might have inflicted far more serious defeats on the Americans, although it is still unlikely that they could have overcome the acute force/space problems presented by operating in North America, especially once the fire-power, transport and logistical dimensions were altered by moving away from the coast with its possibilities for naval co-operation and concentration of strength.

The American War of Independence is sometimes seen as the first modern war. In terms of the politicization of much of the American public there was an obvious contrast with most European warfare of the previous century, but much about the war, for example the weaponry, was conventional. Furthermore, there was little of the emphasis on large armed forces and the mass production of munitions that was to be such an obvious aspect of the 'industrial warfare' of the nineteenth and early twentieth centuries.

CHAPTER FIVE

NAVAL WARFARE

Battle between Swedish and Russian fleets at Svenskund, July 1790, part of a series of clashes in which the two powers sought to dominate the Gulf of Finland. Russia was simultaneously at war with the Turks, unlike in the previous conflict with Sweden in 1741–3, but Gustavus III of Sweden was still unsuccessful.

NAVAL WARFARE

THE EUROPEANS ENJOYED an effective monopoly of long-distance naval strength. There were other naval powers, especially Oman in the Arabian Sea and off the coast of east Africa, but none matched the Europeans. Despite its enormous resources, the strength of its governmental structure and its local naval capability, China was no longer involved in long-range naval activity as it had been in the early fifteenth century. Similarly, neither Japan nor Korea matched their naval activity of the 1590s.

Turkish naval power in the Arabian Sea or off the coast of east Africa was not what it had been in the sixteenth century, but it remained significant in the Black Sea and the Mediterranean. At the turn of the century, the Turks abandoned their traditional dependence on galleys and built a new fleet of sail-powered galleons which carried more cannon. However, they were affected in both the Black Sea and the Mediterranean by the rise of Russia as a naval force. In the first half of the century, the Turks had been able to hold off Christian naval forces in the eastern basin of the Mediterranean. In 1718, off Cerigo, the Turkish fleet had the advantage over an opposing Christian fleet, principally consisting of Venetian warships; the Christians lost nearly 2,000 men.

From the 1770s the Turks were affected in the Mediterranean by the challenge of rising Russian naval power. They were heavily defeated at Cesmé in the Aegean in 1770 and in the Black Sea at the battles of the Dnieper (1788) and Tendra (1790). In 1790 the British feared that the Russians would be able to send a fleet to

War canoes were important in many regions, on inland waterways (rivers, lakes, swamps), in coastal waters, and in island groups, as in the Pacific. In Africa they were important on rivers such as the Niger and Senegal, as well as on coastal lagoons. Such shallow-draft vessels were inexpensive, quick, manoeuvrable and beachable.

the Red Sea via Madagascar in order to open up a new sphere of naval operations against the Turks.

The naval strength of the north African powers – Morocco, Algiers, Tunis and Tripoli – consisted essentially of privateering forces, appropriate for commerce raiding, but not for fleet engagements. The Moroccans captured the crew of a Dutch frigate in 1751, but only after it had been driven ashore during a storm. European powers dispatched expeditions to show the flag and deter the north Africans from privateering – for example, the French show of force under Joseph de Bauffremont in 1766 – but these had little lasting effect. Occasionally, privateering bases were attacked, but they generally proved difficult targets. In 1784, when a large Spanish fleet attempted to destroy the privateering base of Algiers, a line of Algierian warships prevented the Spaniards from coming inshore. An earlier attack in 1775 had been repelled on land when exposed Spanish troops were subjected to heavy fire and their artillery was delayed by the coastal sand. The French bombardment of the Moroccan privateering bases of Larache and Salé in 1765 achieved little.

In India, Mysore and, more particularly, the Marathas had a measure of naval strength, but they were cut short by British action (against the Marathas in 1755

Dutch fleet and Barbary ships. Attacks by the Barbary states of North Africa, especially Algiers, led the Dutch to send men-of-war twice yearly to escort merchantmen to Italy and the Near East. In addition, there were efforts to show the flag and to chase privateers. Formal conflicts included war with Algiers in 1716–26 and 1755–9, and with Morocco in 1751–2 and 1774–7.

BUKHARA

Amu Darya

60°

• Faizabad

• Kabul

KASHMIR

C H I N A

AFGHANISTAN

• Rawalpindi

Indus

T i b e t

• Kandahar

Lahore

• Lahore

Ladakh

Chenab

Ravi

30°

• Quetta

Punjab

Sutlej

BALUCHISTAN

Multan

50°

40°

• Lhasa

Brahmaputra

RAJPUTANA

• Delhi

• Rampur

N E P A L

S i k k i m

B h u t a n

Sind

Indus

• Jodhpur

Ganges

1803

Agra

OUDH

1801

• Ajmer

1801

Lucknow

• Kathmandu

• Hyderabad

• Karachi

Bihar

Benares

1764

Bengal

1775

1764

Ganges

1757

• Dacca

Tropic of Cancer

Chandernagore

• Calcutta

1805

MARATHA

Gujerat

CONFEDERACY

1803

Nagpur •

Arabian Sea

Diu

20°

Daman

1805

Cuttack

Bay of Bengal

1805

Godavari

Bombay •

Nizam's Dominions

to 1805

1766

• Hyderabad

India: rise of British
power 1700–1805

1786

• Janaon

English bases in 1700

French bases in 1700

Goa

1800

Portuguese bases in
1700

1801

Dutch bases in 1700

1800

1799

Mysore

1801

1760

• Madras

British victory, with
date

Mangalore •

Bangalore •

1753

British gains 1756–67

Seringapatam •

1792

C a r n a t i c

• Pondicherry

British gains 1768–85

Mahé •

• Carical

1792

1799

□ Negapatam

British gains 1786–93

Laccadive Is.

10°

1799

British gains 1794–1805

Cochin •

Travancore

Palk Strait

• Jaffna

States under subsidiary
alliance with Britain

1801

N

*Gulf of
Mannar*

1799

Date of gain or
alliance

Maldive Is.

Ceylon
(Dutch)

• Kandy

0   200 km

Colombo •

0   200 miles

I N D I A N   O C E A N

and against Mysore in 1783), when, as John Macpherson of the East India Company noted, the British took the ports belonging to Tipu Sultan, 'in some of which we have found the materials and great advancement of a very considerable naval power'. Further east, there were important regional naval powers in the East Indies. The Illanos of the Sulu Islands deployed large fleets of heavily armed galleys, more appropriate for inshore operations than the deeper-draught sailing ships. They were able and willing to attack the warships of the Dutch East India Company. The Buginese state of Bone also mounted major raids by sea, and in the 1720s and 1730s a Bugi pirate of royal descent, Arung Singkang, conquered part of east Borneo.

European navies continued the pattern of development begun in the mid seventeenth century with a concentration on specialized warships instead of armed merchantmen, numbers, organization and infrastructure; they also increased naval fire-power and devised line-ahead tactics for warships. These were interlinked and mutually sustaining changes, whose net effect was an increase in naval force. Fire-power was enhanced by the replacement of bronze cannon with cast-iron guns which were cheaper and sufficiently dependable to replace the much more expensive, but also lighter, bronze guns. Heavier shot was fired and the fire-power of many individual ships of the line now surpassed that of entire armies. English broadside fire-power increased with the development of improved tackles which used the gun's recoil to speed reloading inboard. Navies became specialized fighting forces. The Dano-Swedish war of 1675–9 was the last in European waters in which armed merchantmen were used extensively in the main battle fleets. Shipbuilding techniques had also improved around this time.

The growth in European naval power was not simply a matter of developments afloat. New naval bases were created and existing ones enhanced, so that a new geography of naval power, based on ports such as Brest and Plymouth, was created. Both these ports had direct access to the Atlantic, which became more important to Britain and France than locations on the North Sea and the Mediterranean.

The major expansion of Russian naval power under Peter the Great was linked to the foundation of St Petersburg as capital, 'window to the west' and port on Russia's newly conquered Baltic coastline. In 1703 Peter himself laid the foundation stone of the Peter–Paul Fortress. The following year he founded the Admiralty Shipyard on the bank of the river Neva opposite the fortress, and in 1706 its first warship was launched. A naval academy followed in 1715. By 1720 Russia was the strongest naval power in the Baltic. Baltic naval conflict is an example of a much overlooked aspect of naval warfare: variety. Alongside clashes between deep-draught warships, there were also engagements between galley fleets. In 1719 Russian galley-borne forces ravaged the eastern coast of Sweden. Galleys were particularly useful in shallow and island-strewn waters such as those in the Gulf of Finland, the approach to St Petersburg.

Lake, lagoon and river warfare could also be important. Thus, in 1702, the

INDIA, RISE OF BRITISH POWER

The British were greatly aided by divisions among their opponents, but the establishment of British power was a difficult process, especially in south and west India. The decisive successes there did not come until after 1790.

OVERLEAF: *Clash between Barbary privateers and Venetian squadron, 19 April 1756. Peace with the Turks from 1718 encouraged a reduction of the Venetian fleet, and it essentially served to protect trade. The Turks also reduced their navy, but in 1770 had to face the Russian navy in the Aegean. This is an example of the role of northern European powers in the Mediterranean that had begun with the English and Dutch.*

Swedish flotilla on Lake Ladoga was defeated by a far larger Russian squadron; in 1776 the British and the Americans clashed on Lake Champlain, and in 1812–14 on Lake Erie. Outside Europe, European warships, with their deep draughts, wooden hulls and reliance on wind power, were of little value in the generally shallow estuary, delta and river waters, and also in many coastal areas.

The Comte de Maurepas, the French minister of the marine 1723–49, described a naval battle: 'two squadrons go out of two hostile ports; they manoeuvre, meet, get out some cannon-shots, knock down some masts, tear some sails, kill some men, use a great deal of powder and cannon balls, then each … retires … they both claim victory … and the sea remains no less salty'. Later in the century, John Jervis, a British admiral, wrote to the secretary of the Admiralty: 'I have often told you, that two fleets of equal force never could produce decisive events, unless they are equally determined to fight it out; or the commander-in-chief of one of them misconducts his line.'

Despite these limitations, greater naval capability encouraged the projection

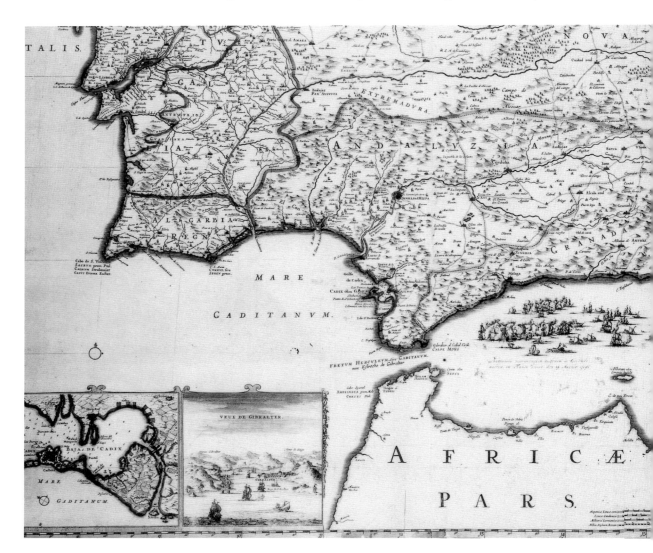

of naval power. A large English fleet was dispatched to the Mediterranean in 1694 and wintered at Cadiz. The English fleet played a major role in the Mediterranean in the War of the Spanish Succession, attacking Toulon (1707), covering the capture of *Minorca* (1708) and Sardinia (1708), and supporting English forces in Spain. In 1713 the British navy carried their ally Victor Amadeus II of Savoy-Piedmont and 6,000 of his troops to take possession of Sicily. In 1718 a decisive British victory off Cape Passero in Sicily thwarted Spain's plans to regain an Italian empire.

Naval warfare thus could be decisive. Linear tactics were adapted to maximize fire-power: warships could not fire straight ahead, so were deployed to fire broad-sides against a parallel line of opposing vessels. The essential resilience of wooden ships ensured that they were difficult to sink by gunfire (although they would sink if the magazine was detonated), but cannon firing at short range could devastate rigging and masts and effectively incapacitate the ships. So battles in which no ships were sunk could, nevertheless, be both hard fought and decisive. Thus the battle of Rügen between the Danish and Swedish fleets in 1715 left the Danes able to cut supply lines to Stralsund, the last Swedish base in Germany. The French were unable to repair damage sustained in the action off Porto Novo in 1759, so leaving the British in command of Indian waters. The confused nature of many naval engagements was captured by Samuel Bentham, then serving with the Russian navy in the Black Sea, who wrote of an attack by gunboats on 29 June 1788 on some Turkish ships aground near Kinburn:

> We had about as much discipline on our manoeuvres as a London mob. We advanced as many of us as chose immediately, and the rest by degrees till we came within musquet shot of the ships on shore. I with 3 or 4 more got close to 3 of them: where as every one did the best for himself, I continued to place myself on the quarter of the largest and so as to be sheltered by the same from the guns of the one next to it. In this position (as near as I could keep myself where the current ran strong) I remained for I suppose about two hours: firing about 130 shots out of 4 guns. My companions soon left me, as I suppose to go to fight elsewhere: and some others, one or two at a time, came in their places: but the smoke was so great, that I could see only the vessels I was engaged with.

Battle of Malaga, 13 August 1704. Holding the weather gauge, an Anglo-Dutch fleet of fifty-three ships under Sir George Rooke protected Gibraltar from a fifty-strong French fleet under the Count of Toulouse. A gap in the allied line between van and centre closed before the French could exploit it. No ships were sunk, casualties were heavy on both sides, and the Allied fleet ran short of ammunition. Toulouse wanted to renew the battle the next day, but his council of war forced him to return to Toulon. This was the last major battle in the war, and thereafter the Allied fleet held the initiative in the Mediterranean.

Once captured, Gibraltar became a major British naval base. It separated the French fleets based in Brest and Toulon and kept watch on the Spanish base of Cadiz. French squadrons that threatened Gibraltar were destroyed in Gibraltar Bay in October 1704 and March 1705. In 1705 the English fleet supported the successful siege of Barcelona.

Many battles were clearly decisive on the day itself, but the French, who were victorious over an Anglo–Dutch fleet at Beachy Head (1690), failed to exploit their victory. The English were the decisive victors at Barfleur/La Hogue (1692), which ended the threat of a French invasion of England that year. After the somewhat indecisive battle of Malaga (1704) enabled the British to consolidate their newly won position at Gibraltar, the French navy did not challenge the British again until 1744: the age of British naval hegemony had clearly begun and in 1747 two victories off Cape Finisterre revealed that the French navy was unable to protect its long-distance trade. This commercial dimension was another potentially decisive factor: an ability to wreck the foreign trade of rivals could cripple their imperial system and greatly hamper their economy. Even if it was not possible to inflict this degree of damage, higher insurance premiums, danger money for sailors and the need to resort to convoys and other defensive measures could push up the cost of trade. Largely thanks to the British, nearly 1,800 ships and barges insured at Marseilles were captured in the War of the Spanish Succession, a major blow to the French economy. Vessels were seized by warships and by privateers – private vessels given licences to take enemy ships.

Privateers were smaller and less heavily gunned than ships of the line, but they were more manoeuvrable and of shallower draught, and were thus more appropriate for commerce raiding. The major role of privateers and of light warships – frigates, sloops, ketches, etc. – is a reminder of the danger of concentrating on ships of the line, and battles, in any account of naval history.

The analogous situation is that of the major role of light cavalry in raiding, cutting communication routes and challenging any notion of control. To press the analogy further, the limited effectiveness of countermeasures – fortified bases and lines against light cavalry, and blockades and amphibious operations against privateer bases – can be noted. French bases, especially St Malo and Dunkirk, proved difficult to contain and the British suffered greatly from the *guerre de course* (privateering war). Britain's military system was tested in the clash with similar forces – in the struggle with France, sepoy armies in India, regular armies in the Low Countries and battle-fleets on the seas of the world; at the same time, it was also up against dissimilar forces, and the ability to overcome this challenge was crucial to Britain's military success.

Britain's relative success against Bourbon privateers owed much to the size of the navy. Thanks to the capture of enemy ships and to shipbuilding, in 1760 it had a displacement of about 375,000 metric tonnes, at that point the largest navy in the world. The thesis of the contemporary historian Edward Gibbon, that a similarity in weaponry would prevent any one European power from achieving a position of hegemony, was completely inaccurate as far as the maritime and extra-European world was concerned, for the British navy was in fact very similar to its opponents in the weaponry it employed. Sir Thomas Slade, Surveyor of the British Navy, 1755–71, working from Spanish and French warships captured in the 1740s, designed a series of two-decker 74-gun warships that were both manoeuvrable and capable of holding their own in the punishing close-range artillery duels of line of battle engagements.

European powers frequently copied each others' developments. This copying could take the form of hiring foreign shipwrights and designers, as with Peter the Great's reliance on Dutch and English workers, and of purchasing foreign warships. In the mid 1780s the Turks employed French experts on ship construction.

In overseas conflict, the British used weapons and tactics similar to those of their European rivals, and they benefited from the general increase in long-distance naval capability that stemmed in part from changes in ship design. A gap in weaponry capability was not therefore responsible for British success. The greater effectiveness of the British navy was largely due to the fact that it had more ships, to its extensive and effective administrative system, to the strength of public finances and to good naval leadership; Britain had a more meritocratic promotion system and more unified naval tradition than that of France, and a greater commitment of national resources to naval rather than land warfare, a political choice that reflected the major role of trade and the national self-image. This contrasted greatly with China, and thus the two strongest powers of the period, both of which greatly expanded territorially around 1760, were very different politically, geopolitically, and militarily. The French financial system lacked the institutional strength and stability of its British counterpart, and this badly affected French naval finances in 1759. The French also lacked an effective chain of naval command and trade was less important to their government and their political culture.

The British naval position had been challenged by the Bourbons in the period 1746–55, as the total displacement tonnage of warships launched during these years by the Bourbons was nearly three times that launched by the British. Fortunately for Britain, Spain did not join the Seven Years War (1756–63) until 1762, and by then France had been defeated at sea. The crucial campaign was that of 1759. The leading French minister, Choiseul, planned a naval concentration to cover an invasion of Britain, prefiguring the strategy of Napoleon. However, the division of the French navy between the distant bases of Brest and Toulon made this concentration difficult and, as in the Trafalgar campaign of 1805, the blockading British squadrons endeavoured to maintain the division. Again, as in 1805, it was easier for the British to maintain the blockade of nearby Brest and less easy to control more distant squadrons. The Toulon fleet under La Clue managed to leave first the harbour and then the Mediterranean, but it was pursued by Edward Boscawen and attacked near Lagos on the Portuguese coast on 18 August 1759. Stubborn resistance by the rearmost French warship, the *Centaure*, held off the British, while La Clue brought the rest of his fleet into neutral waters, but on the next day Boscawen violated Portuguese neutrality and launched a successful attack. Mortally wounded, La Clue ran his vessel ashore and burnt it to prevent it being taken by the British; the outnumbered French lost a total of five ships.

Bad weather forced Edward Hawke, the leading practitioner of close blockade, to lift his blockade of Brest in November, but the Brest fleet under Conflans failed in its attempt to reach Scotland via the west coast of Ireland. Trapped by Hawke while still off the Breton coast, Conflans took refuge in Quiberon Bay, counting on its rock-strewn waters and strong swell to deter Hawke's ships. The British had little knowledge of the rocks in the bay, and it was far harder for sailing ships to operate safely inshore than it would later be for steamships, which were better able to hold their position in the face of strong winds. Nevertheless, on 20 November 1759 the determined Hawke made a bold attack. With topsails set, despite the ferocity of the gale, which blew at nearly forty knots, his ships overhauled the French rear division and forced a general action, in which British gunnery and seamanship proved superior and seven French ships were captured, wrecked or sunk. All possibility of a major French invasion of Britain was now gone and the British were confirmed in their view that they were *the* naval power.

This view was to be challenged in the next war, the American War of Independence. Thanks to much shipbuilding in the late 1760s and 1770s, especially by Spain, then one of the most dynamic states in Europe, by 1780 France and Spain combined had a quantitative superiority in naval tonnage over Britain of about 25 per cent. Partly as a result, the British were unable to repeat their success of the Seven Years War.

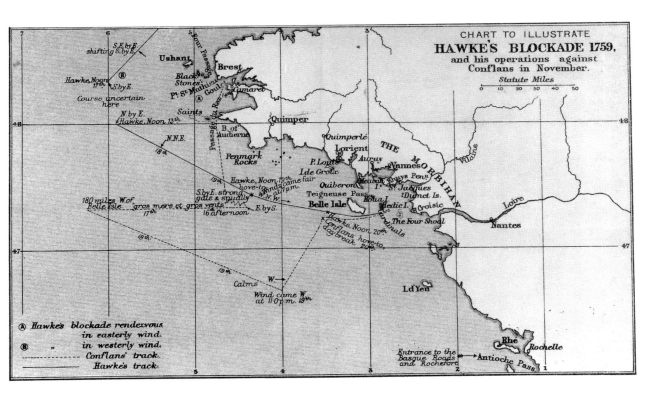

CHART TO ILLUSTRATE
HAWKE'S BLOCKADE 1759,
and his operations against
Conflans in November.

The British navy had control of neither European nor American waters, and it was unable to defeat the French before Spain entered the war – on 17 July 1778 Augustus Keppel failed in his attempt to destroy the Brest fleet off Ushant. British naval strength was concentrated on defending home waters, so Toulon was not blockaded and the Toulon fleet was able to sail to American waters and threaten New York in 1778. The following year, France and Spain sent a fleet into the Channel; this attempt to invade Britain was thwarted by disease and poor organization rather than by British naval action. The British position in the West Indies was also challenged.

It was not until the battle of the Saints on 12 April 1782 that there was a decisive British naval victory to rank with Lagos and Quiberon Bay. It was a testimony to the rising importance of colonies and transoceanic operations, and the failure of the British to maintain an effective blockade, that this battle was fought in the Caribbean, off the Iles des Saintes, south of Guadeloupe. The outnumbered French, under their commander, François de Grasse, were soundly defeated by George Rodney, who broke through the French line, capturing five ships of the line, including the flagship, the *Ville de Paris*, with de Grasse himself. This was a great British achievement. Although there were thirty-six British ships of the line against thirty French ships, the French ships were larger and the total displacements of the two fleets were roughly equal; in most fleet actions, the number of ships of the line present tends to overestimate British and under-estimate French strength as French ships were on average larger than the British. The same applies to number of cannon, as the French pound was heavier than the

Battle of Quiberon Bay, 20 November 1759. The Brest squadron escaped late in the year, but was delayed by the need to join with transports and by contrary winds, giving Sir Edward Hawke an opportunity to attack in a high wind.

*Battle of Quiberon Bay,
20 November 1759. British
gunnery and seamanship
proved superior in this
confused engagement, and
seven French ships of the
line were captured, sunk or
wrecked.*

Battle of the Glorious First of June 1794. Richard, Earl of Howe, with twenty-five ships of the line successfully attacked a French fleet of twenty-six of the line sent to escort a grain convoy from America. Howe, who had gained the weather gauge through skilful seamanship, could not fully execute his plan for all his ships to cut

British and the larger French ships had 36-pounders against British 32-pounders. However, the British gradually obtained a qualitative advantage in cannon.

The French commander in the Indian Ocean, Pierre-André Suffren, was more successful than de Grasse, fighting Edward Hughes in a series of engagements in the Bay of Bengal in 1782–3. Peace came in 1783, but it was not convincing. Five years later, Cornwallis wrote about a possible attack on the French in Pondicherry: 'unless we have a fleet capable of looking the enemy in the face, we must not hazard a considerable body of troops'.

The relative success of the Bourbons encouraged a naval race in the 1780s, when they and Britain both launched a formidable amount of tonnage. These

huge naval forces dwarfed those of non-European powers far more decisively than they had when Christopher Columbus and Vasco da Gama sailed forth in the 1490s. Some other powers also greatly expanded their navies in the 1780s: Russia became the fourth leading power and the Dutch, who had been in that position, or higher, until the early 1750s (before dropping to fifth in 1755–65 and to sixth in 1775–80), expanded their navy to regain, with a greater size than before in that century, the fifth position from 1785. Denmark, Sweden, Naples, Portugal and the Turks also all increased the size of their navies. Sweden and Russia fought a series of bitter naval engagements in the Baltic in 1788–90 as Gustavus III attempted, unsuccessfully, to win back territory lost to the Russians in 1743.

the French line, each passing under the stern of a French ship and engaging it from leeward, but enough ships succeeded; superior British gunnery was at close range for long enough to cost the French seven warships (one sunk, six captured) and 5,000 casualties; the vital convoy, however, reached France.

Battle between Swedish and Russian fleets at Skargard, 1790. Gustavus III of Sweden was committed to his navy and developed it as a force against Catherine the Great of Russia. However Russia held off the Swedish attack in 1788–90.

Programmes of naval construction indicated not only the resources of European governments, but also the capability of their military–industrial complexes. For example, progress in British metallurgy improved their gunnery towards the end of the century, and the impact of British naval gunfire on enemy hulls and crews markedly increased during the war period 1793–1815, when enemy ships were reduced to wrecks in a comparatively short time. Britain had an advantage in technology as well as having good seamanship and well-drilled gun crews.

Fleets of warships were powerful and sophisticated military systems, sustained by mighty industrial and logistical resources based in dockyards that were among the largest industrial plants, employers of labour and groups of building in the world. These dockyards were supported by massive storehouses, such as the vast Lands Zeemagazijn in Amsterdam, which was destroyed by fire in 1791. Naval bases required considerable investment. In 1784 a British diplomat reported of the newly begun French base at Cherbourg: 'The mole is to consist of fourscore immense cases of a conical form, filled with stones, and to be sunk close to each other. The expense of every one of these cases is estimated at near twelve thousand pounds.' Already, in the age of sail, these military–industrial complexes had a capacity for change. There were numerous innovations, which were put to good use. Improvements in seaworthiness, stemming in part from the abandonment of earlier top-heavy and clumsy designs, increased the capability of warships both to take part in all-weather blockades and to operate across the oceans. Furthermore, after the War of American Independence, the French adopted recent British naval innovations, such as the copper-sheathing of ships' bottoms in order to discourage barnacles and so increase manoeuvrability; there was also the new powerful short-range cannon, the carronade, a gun named after the Scottish ironworks where it was manufactured. Standardization was increasingly apparent in the period, and in 1786 the French adopted standard ship designs for their fleet.

A similar pattern can be discerned in another sphere of intense naval competition, the Baltic. There developments in ships of the line were mirrored by the improvement of galleys designed to operate among the archipelagos in the Gulf of Finland. In 1788–90 the Swedo-Russian war there saw each side attempting to match or thwart the naval capability of the other. The Swedish ship designer, Fredrik Henrik af Chapman, had studied in France and Britain. He developed oared archipelago frigates whose diagonal internal stiffenings enabled them to carry heavy guns in a light, shallow-draught hull, and oared

gunboats, small boats with great fire-power and a small target area; the guns were moved on rails and used as ballast when the boats sailed in open waters. In 1788–90 both navies constructed a large number of oared vessels, but, while Sweden concentrated on gunboats, the Russians built a large number of oared frigates as well. The battles of 1790 would demonstrate that the gunboat was the better solution.

The Europeans also took their naval military–industrial capability abroad, with major shipyards at colonial bases such as Havana and Halifax. In the West Indies the British had two naval bases on Jamaica – Port Royal and Port Antonio – as well as English Harbour on Antigua, begun in 1728. Port Royal was able to careen the larger ships of the line sent there. The growing British naval and mercantile presence in the Indian Ocean owed much to shipyards in India, where merchantmen were constructed, averaging 600–800 tonnes and capable of carrying very large cargoes.

A somewhat fanciful illustration of the first use of a submarine in war, the Turtle, *designed by David Bushnell and manned by Ezra Lee, attacking off Staten Island, 6–7 September 1776. Serious problems were encountered with navigating in the face of the currents and the charge could not be attached. The second attempt, on 5 October 1776, also failed. The* Turtle *was spotted and the target was lost.*

Overseas naval forces supported European trade. In 1725 when French merchants were expelled from their base at Mahé on the west coast of India, the French sent a squadron from Pondicherry, forcing the return of the merchants and obtaining new commercial benefits. Moves against French trade at the coffee port of Mocha in Yemen led to the dispatch of a squadron from Pondicherry in October 1736. Arriving off Mocha the following January, the French bombarded the port, disembarked troops and seized the port, thereby restoring their commercial privileges. European navies organized the charting of much of the world's coastlines, to the benefit of trade as well as the assertion of power. For example, in 1764–81 George Gauld was instructed by the British Admiralty to chart the waters of the Gulf of Mexico, a means to consolidate the recent acquisition of Florida. However, naval operations outside Europe, especially in the Indian Ocean and the Caribbean, remained greatly dependent on climate and

disease. Despite improvements in some spheres, the general conditions of service at sea remained bleak. Disease led to high mortality, from, for example, yellow fever in the British and Spanish fleets in the 1720s and typhus in the British and Dutch fleets in the 1740s. The situation was exacerbated by cramped living conditions, poor sanitation and inadequate and inappropriate food; in particular there was a shortage of any fresh food, fruit or vegetables, and hence no vitamin C. The cumulative impact was both to make naval service unattractive and to ensure serious losses among those already in service.

Britain and France came close to war in the Dutch crisis of 1787 and, this time with Spain on France's side, in the Nootka Sound crisis of 1790. They did not fight again, however, until 1793, by which time the French fleet had been badly affected by the political and administrative disruption stemming from the French Revolution. In 1793 the British were invited into Toulon by French

Capture of St Lucia, February 1762, by Captain Augustus Hervey, husband of the bigamous Duchess of Kingston and, later, Third Earl of Bristol. The defeat of the French navy left their island possessions vulnerable to British amphibious attack. In 1762 Hervey went on to take part in the capture of Havana. In 1779 he attacked the state of the navy in the House of Lords.

Royalists, before being driven out again by revolutionary forces benefiting from the well-sited cannon of Napoleon, then a young artillery officer. The following year the British defeated France's Brest fleet at the battle of the Glorious First of June. The British had grasped the controlling maritime position, only to see it collapse in 1795–6, when the French forced the Spanish and the Dutch into alliance and gained the benefit of their fleets, forcing the vulnerable British to evacuate the Mediterranean. Once more able to threaten invasion, the French confronted Britain in a struggle for her survival in 1797–8 and 1805, a struggle the result of which was decisive in the defeat of the attempt to subvert Europe to one hegemonic power and, ultimately, to the destructive will of one man.

Much of this book owes its novelty and importance to a determination to contextualize European developments and to give due weight to non-European powers and peoples. At sea, however, there was no balance, no frontier of capability and control. This was dramatically demonstrated as European warships, under naval commanders such as James Cook, Jean-François de La Pérouse, Antonio Malaspina and George Vancouver, explored the Pacific, on the unknown side of the earth. They established the first European colony in Australasia – the British base at Botany Bay in 1788 – considered where to establish naval bases, charted and (re-)named the world, and in 1790 came close to conflict over trade on what would later be called Vancouver Island. There was still much of the world's land surface where European military strength and European models were unknown, but the warships that ran out their guns around the globe were the forceful edge of the first real integration of the world, an integration made by Europeans and to their own ends and profit.

Battle of the Saints, 12 June 1782. The outnumbered French fleet, commanded by de Grasse, was soundly defeated by George Rodney, who broke through the French line, capturing five ships of the line, including the flagship. British cannon fire was particularly effective thanks to innovations that increased the ease of serving cannon, of firing them instantaneously, and the possible angles of training them.

New Zealand war canoe drawn by Sydney Parkinson who accompanied Captain Cook to the Pacific. His drawings were used for two narratives that appeared in 1773.

CHAPTER SIX

WAR WITHIN EUROPE

A SCENE FROM THE SEVEN YEARS WAR. Such close-quarter combat was less common in battle than this illustration might suggest. A large percentage of wounds was caused by musket balls, not bayonets or swords.

WAR WITHIN EUROPE

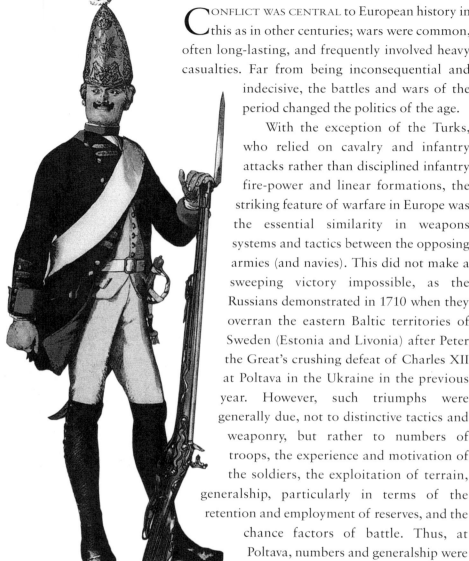

CONFLICT WAS CENTRAL to European history in this as in other centuries; wars were common, often long-lasting, and frequently involved heavy casualties. Far from being inconsequential and indecisive, the battles and wars of the period changed the politics of the age.

With the exception of the Turks, who relied on cavalry and infantry attacks rather than disciplined infantry fire-power and linear formations, the striking feature of warfare in Europe was the essential similarity in weapons systems and tactics between the opposing armies (and navies). This did not make a sweeping victory impossible, as the Russians demonstrated in 1710 when they overran the eastern Baltic territories of Sweden (Estonia and Livonia) after Peter the Great's crushing defeat of Charles XII at Poltava in the Ukraine in the previous year. However, such triumphs were generally due, not to distinctive tactics and weaponry, but rather to numbers of troops, the experience and motivation of the soldiers, the exploitation of terrain, generalship, particularly in terms of the retention and employment of reserves, and the chance factors of battle. Thus, at Poltava, numbers and generalship were crucial: the Swedes suffered terrible casualties, as their brave and foolhardy attack on a well-defended Russian position exposed them to the more numerous Russian infantry and artillery.

A cantonal system of recruitment was established in Prussia between 1727 and 1735. Every regiment was assigned a permanent catchment area around its peacetime garrison town, from which it drew its draftees for lifelong service. For most of the year the troops worked.

New weapons were developed: the socket bayonet and the flintlock musket in the late seventeenth century, the elevating screw for cannon in the eighteenth, as well as the introduction of conic ramrods which allowed the reduction of the difference between the muzzle calibre and the ammunition calibre and thereby promoted more precise targeting. The rapid introduction of successful inventions or modifications in most European armies suggests that the importance of closing technological gaps was well recognized.

The introduction of the socket bayonet helped to change the face of the

European battlefield. Prior to that, infantry had been divided between musketeers and pikemen. The former were more numerous and provided fire-power, but the pikemen were necessary in order to protect the musketeers from cavalry and from other pikemen. The combination of the two was complex and led to a degree of tactical inflexibility as well as a density of formation that limited the possibilities of linear deployment over an extensive front.

Initially, plug bayonets were adopted. They fitted into the muzzle of the barrel, but had to be removed before firing, a process that caused delay and could damage the barrel. However, at the close of the seventeenth century, these were replaced by socket bayonets, which were attached to a metal ring around the

Battle of Poltava, 1709. Striking Russian victory over Charles XII of Sweden. The Swedes suffered terrible casualties as their attack on a well-defended Russian position exposed them to superior forces and artillery. Charles could not grasp control of the battle as he had at Narva in 1700.

barrel. Muskets could now be fired with bayonets in place. By 1697 the majority of English musketeers used socket bayonets; in the 1700s the pike, no longer necessary, disappeared from European armies.

This led to an increase in fire-power and tactical flexibility, as all the infantry were now armed with muskets. The change permitted more effective drill, and drill and discipline were essential to fire-power. More linear infantry formations were employed on the battlefield. Battalions were drawn up only three ranks deep, and firings were by groups of platoons, in a process designed to maximize the continuity of fire and fire-control. The greater battlefield mobility of the infantry put a premium on a more mobile field artillery, and this was achieved during the eighteenth century, with advances being made by the British, Swedes, Austrians, Russians, Prussians and French.

Tactical innovations were also rapidly disseminated, rendering any advantage merely temporary. In 1745 Frederick the Great, the young warrior-king of Prussia (1740–86), developed the attack in oblique order, so as to be able to concentrate overwhelming strength against a portion of the linear formation of the opposing army. Frederick devised a series of methods for strengthening one end of his line

Frederick the Great leading his troops. In practice generals did not usually lead from the front in European warfare. Such conduct would have made it very difficult to exercise command or retain control.

and attacking with it, while minimizing the exposure of the weaker end. This tactic depended on the speedy execution of complex manoeuvres for which well-drilled and well-disciplined troops were essential. It was used to great effect in defeating the Austrians at Leuthen (6 December 1757): Frederick, benefiting from the cover of a ridge, turned the Austrian left flank while a feint attack led the Austrians to send their reserves to bolster their right. The Austrian left crumbled under the oblique attack. However, the Austrians soon developed tactics to thwart the oblique attack, usually by retaining reserves which could be moved to meet the Prussian attack; the tactical gap was thus closed.

Frederick the Great is generally seen as representing the highest point of warfare in the eighteenth century before the French Revolution, but this is misleading, not least because it has led to a neglect of such effective contemporary forces as the Austrians under Count Leopold Daun, the French under Marshal Saxe and the Russians under Rumyantsev. Moreover, in Frederick's last war, the War of the Bavarian Succession with Austria in 1778–9, victory eluded him. In addition, Frederician tactics were most suited to the particular environment of east-central Europe,

SOCKET BAYONETS

These were widely used among the larger German armies by the 1690s. They increased fire-power, but did not greatly encourage attacks because bayonet drills were for a long time based on pike drills, with the weapon held high and an emphasis on receiving advances.

Flintlock Muskets. The British Brown Bess had a large bore ensuring that it could take musket ammunition of any calibre. The loose fit of the ball helped ramming and thus contributed to the rate of fire, but ensured that accuracy was lost with distance. Problems were also caused by the stiff trigger, by powerful recoil, and by poor performance in wet weather if the powder became damp.

especially the unenclosed tracts of Bohemia and Silesia. Their limitations were to be revealed in the French Revolutionary War from 1792, in the face of French troops fighting in open order in the enclosed and wooded country of the Austrian Netherlands and eastern France.

Prior to that conflict, the tactics of European armies had focused on the deployment of infantry in close-packed, thin, linear formations, in order to maximize fire-power. 'After a terrible firing of near half an hour', according to

Battle of Sheriffmuir, 1715, by John Wootton. The Jacobites under John, Earl of Mar, failed to exploit their numerical superiority and, after an indecisive battle, left the government forces under John, Duke of Argyll in possession of the battlefield and with the initiative.

a participant, the French front line retreated before the British at Dettingen (1743). Linear formations also lessened the problems of command and control posed by the limitations of information and communication on the battlefield. Soldiers used flintlock muskets equipped with bayonets, and fired by volley, rather than employing individually aimed shot. Despite the bayonets, hand-to-hand fighting on the battlefield was relatively uncommon and most casualties were caused by shot. The accuracy of muskets was limited, and training, therefore, stressed rapidity of fire, and thus drill and discipline. Musket fire was commonly delivered at close range.

The problems created by short-range muskets, which had a low rate of fire

and had to be re-sighted for each individual shot, were exacerbated by the cumulative impact of poor sights, eccentric bullets, heavy musket droops, recoil, overheating, and misfiring in wet weather. As muskets were smooth bore and there was no rifling, or grooves, in the barrel, the speed of the shot was not high and its direction was uncertain. Non-standardized manufacture and wide clearances (windage) meant that the ball could roll out if the barrel was pointed towards the ground, while, at best, the weapon was difficult to aim or to hold steady. Balls were rough cast and the spherical bullets maximized air resistance. The development of iron, instead of wooden, ramrods was believed to increase the rate of musket fire, but these often bent and jammed in the musket, or broke

or went rusty; and frequent use of the ramrod distorted the barrel into an oval shape.

Despite these failings, because the combatants were densely packed and fought at close range, casualties could be substantial. Low muzzle velocity led to dreadful wounds, because the more slowly a projectile travels the more damage it does as it bounces off bones and internal organs.

The infantry was flanked by cavalry units, but the proportion of cavalry in European armies declined during the century as a result of the heavier emphasis on fire-power and the greater cost of cavalry. Cavalry was principally used on the battlefield to fight cavalry; cavalry advances against unbroken infantry were uncommon, although infantry was vulnerable to attack in flank and rear. At Dettingen, French cavalry attacked British infantry only to be cut to pieces by their fire-power, as a British participant recorded:

George II at the battle of Dettingen, 1743, by John Wootton. The French set a trap for the less numerous British. One part of their army under the Duke of Grammont was deployed in a strong position behind the Dettingen stream, blocking the British route, while another part threatened the British rear. Instead of holding his position, Grammont advanced, only to be driven back by superior British musketry.

They rode up to us with a pistol in each hand, and their broad swords slung on their wrists. As soon as they had fired their pistols they flung them at our heads, clapped spurs and rode upon us sword in hand. The fury of their onset we could not withstand so they broke our ranks and got through; but our men immediately closed [ranks] and turned about, and with the assistance of a regiment ... who were in our rear, the French horse being between both, we killed them in heaps.

Cavalry played a crucial role in some battles, such as the British victory over the French at Blenheim (13 August 1704) and the Prussian over the French at Rossbach (5 November 1757). Cavalry–infantry co-ordination, or at least combination, could be important. At Fraustadt in 1706 a Swedish army under Karl Gustaf Rehnskjold defeated a Saxon force twice its size, the numerous Swedish cavalry enveloping both Saxon flanks, while the relatively small Swedish infantry held off attacks in the centre. In general, however, cavalry was less important than it had been in the past.

Unbroken infantry was more vulnerable to artillery than it was to cavalry, especially because of the close-packed and static formations that were adopted in order to maintain discipline and fire-power. The use of artillery on the battlefield increased considerably during the century, and, by the end of the Seven Years War, Frederick the Great, who had not, initially, favoured the large-scale use of artillery, was employing massed batteries of guns. Cannon became more mobile and standardized: the Austrians in the 1750s and the French, under Jean-Baptiste Gribeauval, from the 1760s were the leaders in this field. The greater standardization of artillery pieces led to more regular fire and thus encouraged the development of artillery tactics away from the largely desultory and random preliminary bombardments of the seventeenth century in favour of more efficient exchanges of concentrated and sustained fire. Artillery was employed on the battlefield both to silence opposing guns and, more effectively, in order to weaken infantry and cavalry units. Grape and canister shot were particularly effective; they consisted of a bag or tin with small balls inside which scattered as a result of the charge, causing considerable numbers of casualties at short range.

Other technological developments proceeded more slowly. Although the first operational use of a submarine occurred in 1776, when the American David Bushnell tried unsuccessfully to sink HMS *Eagle* in New York harbour, it was not followed up; as yet the very bases of successful underwater existence, such as compressed air, did not exist. Experiments with the use of manned balloons for warfare and with the use of rockets in Europe had to wait until the 1790s.

Nevertheless, despite the absence of major technological advances, it is important to note the economic weight underlying European power. The main Russian state arsenal at Tula produced an annual average of nearly 14,000 muskets between 1737 and 1778. In the 1760s the French produced 23,000 muskets annually at Charleville and Saint-Etienne. New gun foundries were established, including those at Woolwich (1716) and Vienna (1747). The Prussian siege-train at Stralsund in 1715 contained eighty 24-pounders and forty mortars. The military strength of the major states rose substantially. The size of the Russian regular army tripled in the last forty years of the century, a period also of rising Russian naval strength; the annual army costs rose from 9.2 million roubles in 1762 to 21 million roubles in 1796, during a period of modest inflation.

The ability to mobilize resources for war reflected the nature of a society: the combination of a cash economy (which provided a basis for taxation),

THE SEVEN YEARS WAR

A major struggle in central Europe that led to no territorial changes and, instead, consolidated the existing situation, thus confirming Prussia's earlier gains.

under-employment and governments that enjoyed great authority over the bulk of the population, although not the social élite, created the context for the major mobilization of manpower for war. This took a variety of forms, including the systems of general conscription (with exemptions) in eastern Europe, but the common element was the assumption that the bulk of the male population would serve if required and on terms that they did not influence, and that their views on the purposes and methods of warfare would not be sought.

Mutinies were rare, and when they occurred, as in the Württemberg army in 1758, they were caused by a serious collapse of trust. Desertion was far more

common and was harshly punished: it was a dangerous protest against often desperate conditions. Force and trickery were frequently employed in recruitment: Prussian recruiters actually kidnapped men from the neighbouring territories, such as Mecklenburg; Frederick II also forced captured troops to serve him. In general, training was harsh, discipline could be brutal and the conditions of service in terms of accommodation, food and pay were poor, although not always worse than those in civilian society.

The lack of interest in the views of soldiers and sailors did not mean that rulers, generals and admirals were oblivious to the condition of their troops and

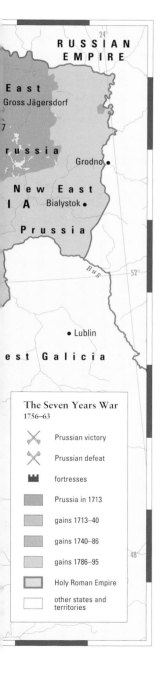

The Seven Years War
1756–63

✕ Prussian victory

✕ Prussian defeat

▟ fortresses

Prussia in 1713

gains 1713–40

gains 1740–86

gains 1786–95

Holy Roman Empire

other states and territories

to casualties. They were well aware that poor food and accommodation could lead to debilitating diseases, although adequate provision was difficult to secure, especially on campaign. The military were a section of the community which governments needed and therefore cared for, albeit at a basic level. Though pay was generally low and was frequently delayed, troops were the largest group paid by governments.

Discipline was not always as savage in practice as it was in theory, a common feature of the law enforcement of the period, which was often tempered and episodic. In the Prussian army only a relatively small number of hard cases received a disproportionate number of the most severe

A battle scene taken from the Seven Years War. Cavalry continued to play a major role on the battlefield, although more against other cavalry than against infantry.

punishments. Although even the most junior officer could inflict harsh penalties, the most vivid accounts of the horrors of Prussian discipline were misleading and selective. Experienced troops could be difficult to replace; new recruits were of limited value until blooded. This could encourage caution in risking battle, although it is necessary not to exaggerate this. The dangers of casualties and defeat did not prevent leaders from seeking battle. There was certainly nothing inherently cautious about generalship at this time. The ethos of the period placed a great premium on bravery and boldness in command, on land and at sea. Although administrative aspects of command, such as recruitment and logistics, were known to be of great consequence, they did not determine the culture of warfare; just as the character of the domestic rule of kings was not decided by the financial issues that they knew to be important. Monarchs were expected to win glory through victory and conquest.

There is a widely held but largely misleading view that warfare before the French Revolution was inconsequential in its results and limited in its methods, and contrasted with the supposed nature of revolutionary warfare. Such a thesis is mistaken. It is difficult to see how, say, the clearing of the French from northern Italy in 1706, or the Russian advance on Warsaw and then Danzig (Gdansk) in 1733–4, can be seen as inconsequential.

Decisiveness is hard to assess: a decisive outcome of one battle or campaign does not automatically lead to a conclusive result with regard to the war itself. Today, a decisive outcome means weakening or destroying the armed forces of the enemy to such an extent that organized military resistance is no longer feasible. It can only be achieved if one side loses a battle to which it has committed the bulk of its military organization, and if the winning side has the resources available to take full advantage of the enemy's (often temporary) weakness.

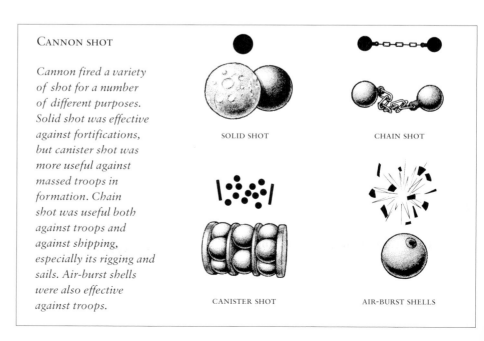

CANNON SHOT

Cannon fired a variety of shot for a number of different purposes. Solid shot was effective against fortifications, but canister shot was more useful against massed troops in formation. Chain shot was useful both against troops and against shipping, especially its rigging and sails. Air-burst shells were also effective against troops.

SOLID SHOT

CHAIN SHOT

CANISTER SHOT

AIR-BURST SHELLS

In the eighteenth century, situations like this did occur, but they were exceptional. Exhaustion, political changes or a gradual deterioration in the strategic balance were much more common reasons for the ending of a war – this was certainly true of the Wars of the Spanish (1701–14), Polish (1733–5), Austrian (1740–48) and Bavarian (1778–9) Successions, and of the Seven Years War in Europe (1756–63).

Yet decisive wars did occur, for example between Sweden and Russia in 1741–3. Furthermore, victories in battle might give rise to political circumstances which led to a negotiated peace: they were decisive in framing the parameters of peace.

Warfare was far from limited. Casualty rates could be extremely high. At Blenheim (1704) there were over 30,000, excluding prisoners, out of the 108,000 combatants; and at Malplaquet (1709), a quarter of the Anglo-Dutch–German force. This

Prussian uniforms, 1786. The war of the Bavarian Succession (1778–9) had revealed serious weaknesses in the Prussian army, despite its high reputation, including the absence of sufficient supplies, demoralized infantry and undisciplined cavalry.

FRENCH FIELD HOWITZER

A French 24-pounder field howitzer c. 1765 designed by Gribeauval, the modernizer of the French artillery.

A German recruiting poster for the Fürstliche Infanterie Regiment Anhalt-Zerbst. This small German principality produced about 500 men for Austrian service in 1761–7.

'butcher's bill' undermined support for the continuation of the war with Louis XIV. The exchange of fire at close quarters (50–80 yards) between lines of closely packed troops, the battlefield use of artillery firing, for example, case-shot against such formations, and cavalry engagements relying on cold steel all produced a large number of casualties. Cornet Philip Brown of the British cavalry wrote of Dettingen, 'the balls flew about like hail', and of Fontenoy, 'I admire and adore that kind Providence who hath been my great protector and preserver of my life and limbs during such a cannonading of nine hours as could not possibly be exceeded ... there were batteries [of cannon] continually playing upon our front and both flanks.'

Aside from such organized savagery, soldiers were often brutal in their treatment of each other and of civilians, although, in general, the treatment of prisoners improved. Nevertheless, the storming of fortifications was sometimes followed by the slaughter of the defenders, as when the French stormed the major

Dutch fortress of Bergen-op-Zoom in 1747. In general, warfare was more savage when regular forces fought irregulars and also in eastern Europe, where religious and ethnic differences increased hatred. However, genocide played no part in the European politics of the age.

Wars had considerable impact on the civilian population. Apart from conflicts involving guerrilla warfare, for example in Hungary, Spain and the Tyrol in the 1700s, the burden of military demands, especially for men and money, pressed hard on the people of Europe. These demands, however, did not challenge the ethos and practice of societies organized around the principles of inegalitarianism and inheritance. Larger armies brought more opportunities to the propertied classes, especially nobles, who benefited from their ability to recruit from their dependants, and from the assumption that they were naturally suited for positions of command – which was usually the case. Thus, armies were not forces 'outside' society, but rather reflections of patterns of social control and

Battle of Malplaquet, 11 September 1709. Marlborough's attack on entrenched French troops under Villars exemplified his belief in the attack, but the French held his attacks on their flanks and retained a substantial reserve to meet his final central push. As before, Marlborough's tactics were based on the acceptance of the likelihood of heavy casualties, but at Malplaquet these casualties did not lead to a rout of the defeated French.

influence, and the beliefs that gave cohesion to them. The roles of patronage and/or purchase were crucial in the appointment of officers. Sir James Lowther noted of the British army in 1742, 'Hardly any rise much in the Army without buying most part of the advances they make, and at the same time selling what they had before. This is the common way, except after hot services and being in such climates as the West Indies where many are carried off.' Such a system greatly limited the pool of talent, and this was to put at a disadvantage forces up against the more egalitarian practices of revolutionary armies in the last quarter of the century.

In the complex balance of punishments and less coercive methods for maintaining discipline and military cohesion, the armed forces again mirrored society; so too did the fact that only men were recruited. No European army matched that of Dahomey in west Africa, which by the 1770s had several hundred women in the standing army. They usually served as the palace bodyguard, although in 1729 and 1781 they went with the king on campaign and by 1850 there were 5,000 female soldiers in the army.

The century began in Europe with two major wars, the Great Northern War (1700–1721) and the War of the Spanish Succession (1701–14). In the former, Frederick IV of Denmark, Peter the Great of Russia and Augustus II of Saxony–Poland planned concerted attacks on the Swedish empire. It was assumed that

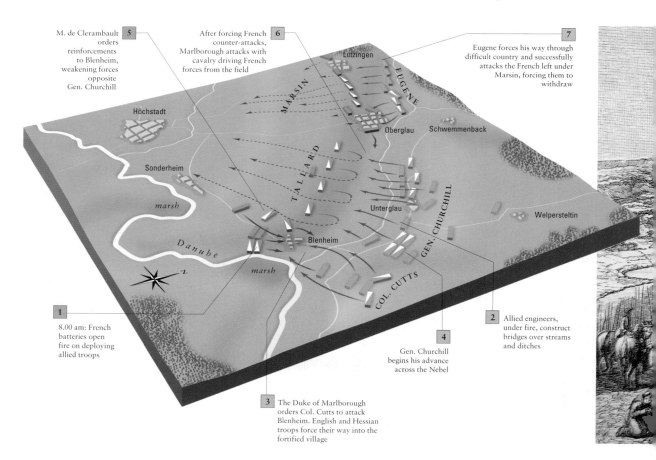

5 M. de Clerambault orders reinforcements to Blenheim, weakening forces opposite Gen. Churchill

6 After forcing French counter-attacks, Marlborough attacks with cavalry driving French forces from the field

7 Eugene forces his way through difficult country and successfully attacks the French left under Marsin, forcing them to withdraw

1 8.00 am: French batteries open fire on deploying allied troops

2 Allied engineers, under fire, construct bridges over streams and ditches

3 The Duke of Marlborough orders Col. Cutts to attack Blenheim. English and Hessian troops force their way into the fortified village

4 Gen. Churchill begins his advance across the Nebel

these attacks would divide the Swedish forces and ensure speedy success. The young Charles XII, however, responded rapidly. A landing on Zealand, threatening Copenhagen, drove Frederick IV out of the war, the strength of Swedish-held Riga's defences blocked Augustus, and Charles was able to move rapidly to Narva in Estonia, which was then being besieged by Peter. The 11,000 Swedes in Charles's army advanced rapidly, giving the more numerous Russians no time to deploy their cannon. Storming the Russian entrenchments in two columns, the Swedes quickly came to hand-to-hand conflict, proving adept with their bayonets. A snowstorm blew directly into the faces of the defenders, and the Russian position collapsed with heavy casualties, 8,000 or 10,000 dead or wounded, compared to only 2,000 Swedes. Peter's new regiments, trained according to German models, as well as his more traditional units,were routed.

Narva (1700) showed that a poorly commanded and badly deployed siege army was vulnerable to a relief attempt; but also, like the campaigns and battles of the War of the Spanish Succession, demonstrated the value of boldness in seizing the initiative. This was also demonstrated in the War of the Spanish Succession by John Churchill, 1st Duke of Marlborough (1650–1722), victor over the French at Blenheim (13 August 1704), Ramillies (23 May 1706), Oudenaarde (11 August 1708) and Malplaquet (11 September 1709). Cool and composed under fire, brave to the point of rashness, Marlborough was a master of the shape

BATTLE OF BLENHEIM, 13 AUGUST 1704

The Duke of Marlborough was more successful than his Franco-Bavarian opponents in shaping the battle, achieving a local superiority in what he made a crucial part of the battlefield. He ably integrated his cavalry and infantry, and brought forward the artillery to support the cavalry breakthrough in the centre. Blenheim destroyed the image of French military superiority.

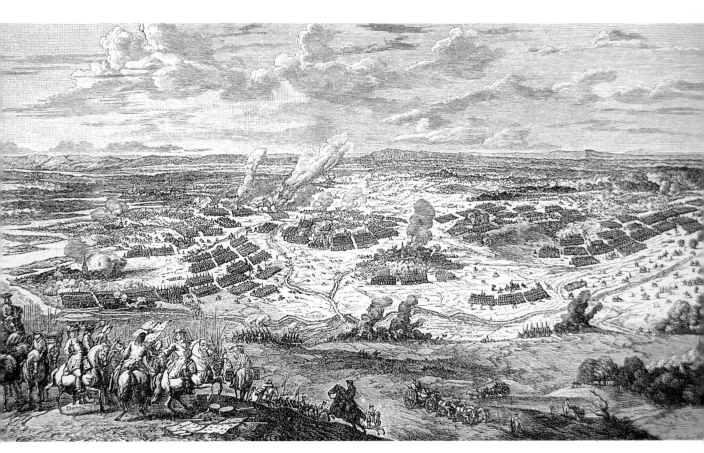

11 211111111111111111111111111111111111111111

Battle of Ramillies, 23 May 1706. A victory thanks to Marlborough's ability to turn an army and a system of operations developed for position warfare into a means to make war mobile. French flanks were tied down before the British smashed through the French centre.

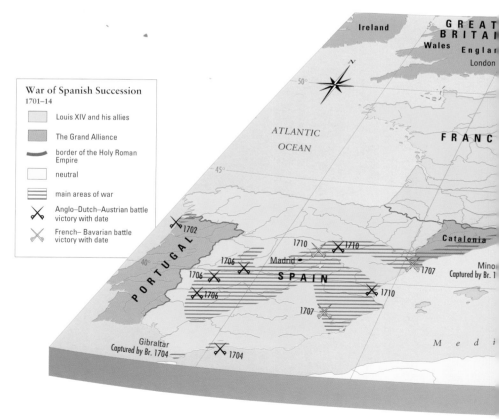

War of Spanish Succession
1701–14

- Louis XIV and his allies
- The Grand Alliance
- border of the Holy Roman Empire
- neutral
- main areas of war
- Anglo–Dutch–Austrian battle victory with date
- French–Bavarian battle victory with date

and the details of conflict. He kept control of his own forces and of the flow of the battle, and was able to move and commit his troops decisively at the most appropriate moment.

In that war, other successful generals revealed the same skills, including the Austrian commander, Prince Eugene, in Italy, and Marshal Berwick, the French commander in Spain. Thus in 1701, 1702 and 1706, Eugene outmanoeuvred and defeated larger French forces in northern Italy, winning the battles of Carpi (9 July 1701), Chiari (1 September 1701), Luzzara (15 August 1702) and Turin (9 September 1706). Berwick, the illegitimate son of James II and Arabella Churchill, and Marlborough's nephew, outmanoeuvred the allied forces in Spain in 1706–7, decisively defeating them at Almanza on 25 April 1707. Such campaigns indicated the importance of moving swiftly, not least in order to disorientate opponents, but such movements depended on a sound grasp of logistics, which both Marlborough and Berwick possessed.

Campaigns, however, did not only proceed by battles; sieges were also important. Fortified positions anchored political power, contained military supplies and controlled communication routes. It was therefore important that Marlborough captured Lille in 1708, Berwick Barcelona in 1714. Sieges had become more formidable undertakings because of advances in fortification technique associated in particular with the French military engineer Sebastien le

WAR OF SPANISH
SUCCESSION IN EUROPE

The struggle over the Spanish succession produced a wide-ranging conflict. Within Europe the French were pushed back from the Low Countries, Germany and Italy, but the Allies failed in Spain.

Prestre de Vauban (1633–1707). Vauban developed the use of bastions, layering in depth, fire and defensive artillery. Such advances, however, would have been of little value without the ability and determination of European governments to spend massive amounts on such fortresses, although it was a period of limited economic growth. Thus, the French developed a series of fortresses to provide defence in depth on their vulnerable north-eastern frontiers. Thanks to these fortresses, Marlborough was unable to translate battlefield victories into the march on Paris which he believed necessary to win the war. The resources used to construct these works were formidable: 1,200–1,500 men worked daily from 1698 to 1705 on the fortress of Neuf-Brisach, part of the French system in the Upper Rhineland, and the supporting infrastructure was formidable. A 40-kilometre canal, including three aqueducts, was constructed to bring materials from the Vosges.

The course of the War of the Spanish Succession reflected, but was not dependent on, the respective strategic strengths of the combatants. France had a relatively secure home base protected by the largest army in western Europe and by excellent fortifications; it was largely immune to British amphibious attack, and was able to suppress the only rebellion that occurred at home, that of the Protestants in the Cevennes. French forces could take the offensive in the Low Countries, Germany, Italy and Spain, and their ability to campaign simultaneously in these areas testified to France's military, fiscal and administrative might.

However, France's opponents were also effective; the British provided financial support and were willing in 1704 to deploy their troops on the Danube, and Marlborough refuted France's claims to military superiority. The Dutch, Austrians, Savoy–Piedmont, Portuguese, and German rulers, such as those of Prussia and Hanover, were also crucial to the anti-French effort, providing forces, soaking up French attacks, and maintaining a united front until the Peace of Utrecht (1713), when Louis XIV was forced to accept terms.

In eastern Europe, where there were far fewer fortifications and no system of advanced fortresses, it was easier for the participants in the Great Northern War to make major advances, as when Charles XII

OPPOSITE: Augustus II, King of Poland 1697–1706, Elector of Saxony, 1709–33. Augustus' hopes that his election to the Polish throne would enable the Saxon dynasty to become a great power were wrecked by the superior generalship of Charles XII of Sweden.

Duke of Marlborough. Skilful in holding the anti-French coalition together and expert in conducting mobile warfare, he brought the British army to a peak of success. He used his cavalry as a massed shock force, handled the artillery well, and maintained continuous fire from his infantry.

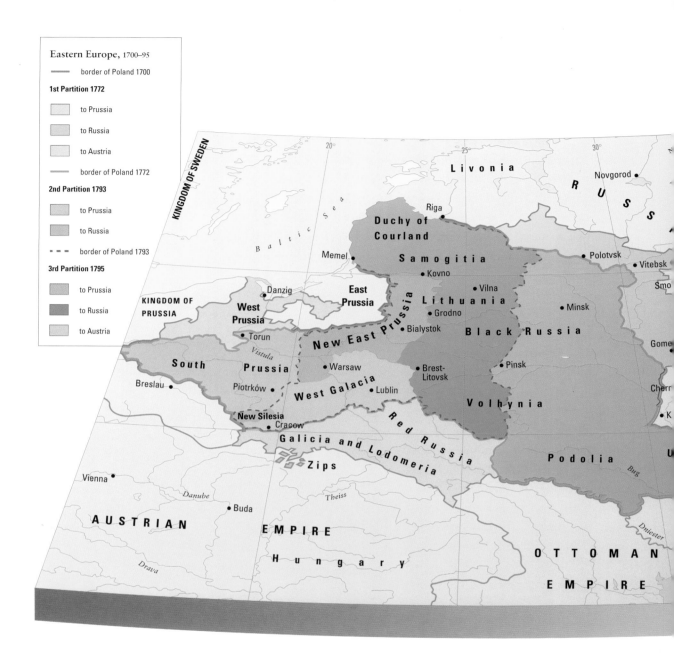

invaded Poland in 1701, Saxony in 1706 and the Ukraine in 1708. However, individual fortresses could be important in eastern Europe, not least as the way to secure control of a region. Thus, the capture of Viborg, Reval, Mitau and Riga in 1710 and of Helsingfors (Helsinki) in 1713 by the Russians, and of Stettin (1714), Stralsund (1715) and Wismar (1716) by Sweden's western assailants, Denmark and Prussia, were crucial stages in the collapse of the Swedish empire. Charles XII himself died while besieging the Norwegian fortress of Fredrikshald in 1718.

Charles's bold, ever-advancing generalship resembled that of Nadir Shah of Persia, rather than the cautious style of some, but by no means all, of his western European counterparts. In 1701 he decided to replace Augustus II of Poland with a more pliable ruler; this led to his being embroiled for some years in the unsteady complexities of Polish politics and diverted him from dealing with the growing power of Peter the Great. In the summer of 1701, under cover of a smokescreen, Charles crossed the River Dvina near Riga, before successfully driving away the defending forces. Charles then overran Courland, before invading first Lithuania and then Poland. He captured Warsaw (March 1702) and Thorn (1703), while Polish–Saxon armies were defeated at Klisów (1702), Pultusk (1703), Punitz (1704) and Fraustadt/Wschowa (1706). The victory at Klisów over a larger Saxon army was typical of Charles's daring generalship, his conviction of the value of the attack and his willingness to take risks. A silent march through difficult terrain secured the element of surprise, the Swedish cavalry attacked at once without pausing to open fire, the artillery was quicker than the more numerous Saxon cannon and the infantry advanced to attack with cold steel in the face of Saxon musket fire. The Saxons broke, as defending forces tended to do if they could not keep their attackers at a distance, and their losses in dead and wounded were at least twice those of the Swedes.

Meanwhile, Peter the Great rebuilt his army. Large numbers of troops were recruited, training improved and the new War Chancellery, established in 1701, improved Russia's logistical capability. A number of victories were won over the Swedes, including Eristfer (1701), Hummelshof (1702), Kalisz (1706), Lesnaia (1708) and, most importantly, Poltava (1709). It is unclear how far these victories can be attributed to Peter's military reforms: superior numbers played a major role, and many of these troops, especially in the battles of 1701–4, were not new-style regiments. Furthermore, the developing Russian metallurgical industry could not meet the army's need for muskets until 1712, so that in 1707 the proportion of pikemen to musketeers was increased, and infantry firearms were not standardized until 1715. The Russian military administration was dogged by confusion, expediency and opportunism.

Yet Peter won. The greater resources of Russia were mobilized by force and thanks to the creation of *gubernii*, super-provinces under governors close to the Tsar, that permitted the creation of an effective governmental system at the regional level. The role of resource availability was shown by the increased importance of the Russian artillery which was greatly developed under Peter; the 102 Russian cannon at Poltava fired 1,471 shots while Charles XII had only four cannon at the battle in which his army was crushed. About 300,000 men were recruited to the army during Peter's reign (1689–1725) and large numbers joined the navy. Annual military expenditure rose

THE FATE OF POLAND

Poland's destruction at the hands of Austria, Prussia and Russia was a brutal demonstration of strength, particularly Russian strength. The partitioning powers were able to organize, control and direct their populations more effectively than Poland. The Partitions were the most significant territorial redistribution in Europe since the 1710s.

from 750,000 roubles in 1680 to 5.4 million roubles in 1724, a year of peace.

The two western European wars after the War of the Spanish Succession – those of the Quadruple Alliance (1718–20) and the Polish Succession (1733–5) – are generally neglected in studies of military history, but they are important in that they show the crucial role of the political contexts and also the variety of warfare in this period. The politics of both wars helped to explain their course. In the War of the Quadruple Alliance, the French government, aware of the unpopularity of war with Spain and unwilling to destroy Spanish power, launched only a limited invasion of northern Spain. Two military successes were important to the course of the conflict: the Spaniards were able to land 20,000 men on Sicily in 1718 and to overrun much of the island, but the British defeat of the Spanish navy in the same year enabled the Austrians to counter-attack (leading to battles such as Francavilla that are generally ignored in works on military history), and the war ended with Spain having to accept Austrian control of Sicily.

In the War of the Polish Succession, France attacked Austria, but signed a neutrality agreement for the Austrian Netherlands (modern Belgium and Luxembourg). France decided not to exploit a successful advance down the Moselle in 1734 by advancing towards Saxony because they did not wish to bring neutral powers, particularly Britain and the United Provinces (Dutch Republic), into the war on the Austrian side. The variety of warfare was well displayed in the same war. Decisive campaigns, such as the Franco-Sardinian invasion of the Austrian-ruled Milan in 1733, the Russian invasion of Poland in the same year and the Spanish invasion of Sicily in 1734, contrasted with those in which only limited advances were made, such as the campaigns in the Rhineland in 1733, 1734 and 1735, and near Mantua in 1735. Decisive battles such as the Spanish defeat of the Austrians at Bitonto on 25 June 1734, which left Spain supreme in southern Italy, contrasted with others where there were no sweeping triumphs or results, such as the engagements between France and Austria at Parma (29 June) and Guastalla (19 September) in northern Italy in 1734.

The War of the Austrian Succession (1740–48) began with a sweeping triumph: Frederick II's conquest of the Austrian province of Silesia (modern south-west Poland), launched in December 1740. This led to the battle of Mollwitz (10 April 1741) in which the Prussian cavalry was ridden down by the more numerous Austrians, causing Frederick to flee, but the well-trained and more numerous Prussian infantry prevailed over their slower-firing opponents, who withdrew after nightfall. It is difficult to ascribe the Prussian success to any superiority in weaponry or generalship; their more numerous infantry – 16,800 to 10,000 – and the fact that many of the Austrians were raw recruits were more important. Mollwitz was not a great triumph; indeed Prussian losses in killed, wounded or missing – 4,800 men – were actually 300 more than those of the Austrians. Had the opportunity arisen for Austria to mobilize its greater strength and concentrate on Frederick he would have been hard pressed, but, as ever, the political context was crucial. In 1741 Maria Theresa of Austria was also attacked

by France, Bavaria and Saxony, while her system of alliance collapsed. Franco-Bavarian forces advanced towards Vienna, before storming Prague in concert with Saxon troops. But again strategy was overthrown by politics: Saxony and Prussia abandoned their allies, and the Austrians, ignoring the maxim that indecisive *ancien régime* warfare avoided winter campaigns, struck back, capturing Linz in January 1742 and Munich the following month. The French besieged Prague that December.

In 1743, George II of Britain entered the war on the Austrian side, leading the troops that defeated the French near Dettingen (17 June): the French had set a trap for the British, but part of their army then abandoned a strong defensive position and advanced, only to be gunned down. George, however, was unable to exploit his victory in order to penetrate France's well-fortified eastern frontier. When the Austrians under Prince Charles of Lorraine invaded Alsace in the

Siege of Ypres, 1744. When the French invaded the Austrian Netherlands they rapidly captured Dutch-garrisoned fortresses such as Furnes, Knocke, Menin and Ypres, which were in poor condition after decades of neglect. Ypres capitulated to Louis after a nine-day siege. He was accompanied by his mistress, the Duchesse de Châteauroux. This illustration dramatizes the heavy bombardment used by the French.

Battle of Fontenoy, 11 May 1745. Louis XV points to the victor, Marshal Saxe. The Duke of Cumberland's use of the direct approach fell victim to Saxe's clever exploitation of the advantages of resting on the defensive. Saxe deployed his reserves effectively. The British infantry displayed their discipline and fire control.

following year, they were soon recalled, as Frederick II had re-entered the war and captured Prague. In 1745 the Austrians, with Saxon support, took the offensive against Frederick, but they were defeated at Hohenfriedberg, Soor, Hennersdorf and Kesselsdorf, by a combination of effective Prussian commanders, flexible tactics and fighting quality. Hohenfriedberg and Soor were victories for what has been termed the oblique attack. Marshal Saxe, the French commander, claimed in 1749 that the Prussian army was only trained to attack and, by retaining the strategic and tactical initiatives, they were able to do so.

The Austrians ended their war with Prussia at Christmas 1745, but by then the French had overrun much of the Austrian Netherlands and defeated an Anglo-Dutch-German counter-attack at Fontenoy (11 May 1745): the Duke of Cumberland, third son of George II, had none of Marlborough's finesse and, instead of enveloping his opponents, was himself enveloped as he launched frontal attacks on prepared positions. In the last of these, Cumberland's troops advanced in rectangular formation, breaking the first French line and defeating the French guards with heavy musket fire; however, the earlier failure to capture the French redoubts on the flanks led to the eventual failure of this attack. The French commander, Marshal Saxe, had deployed his reserves effectively. Although Cumberland's infantry beat off successive attacks by the French cavalry, the French infantry – which was not held down by flank attacks as it would have been on a Marlborough battlefield – redeployed to attack the flanks of Cumberland's column; cannon were also fired into the flanks. Attacked and under fire from

TACTICAL FORMATIONS

In his search for more effective tactical formations, Marshal Saxe placed emphasis on shock action and also deployed light artillery to increase the fire-power of his forces. Saxe advocated the use of light infantry skirmishing ahead of the main force.

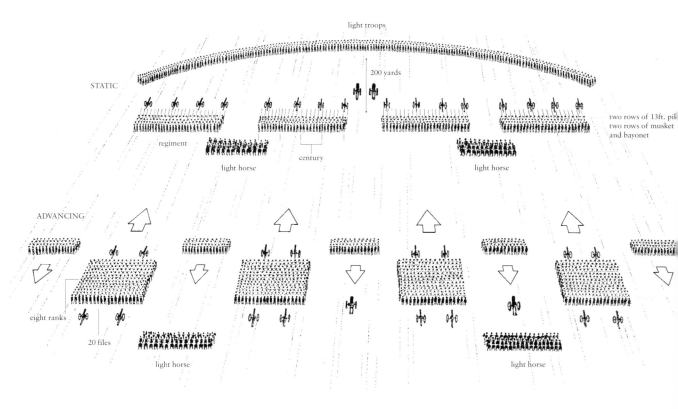

three sides, the British troops withdrew. Napoleon later suggested that the French victory at Fontenoy prolonged the French *ancien régime* monarchy in France by thirty years. Cumberland was to defeat the Jacobite army under Bonnie Prince Charlie (Charles Edward Stuart) at Culloden the following year, but there he had the advantages of superior fire-power, an excellent site and a foolish opponent.

Saxe – who emulated Marlborough in his preference for bold manoeuvres, his emphasis on gaining and retaining the initiative, his ability to control large numbers effectively in battle and his stress on morale – pressed on to win victory for Louis XV in the Low Countries at Roucoux (11 October 1746) and Lawfeldt (2 July 1747), before advancing into the United Provinces and capturing Maastricht (7 May 1748).

Further south, in the last major conflict in Italy prior to the French Revolutionary War, Franco-Spanish forces failed in 1743–4 to break through the alpine defences of the kingdom of Sardinia, the most important possessions of which were Piedmont and Savoy. Politics offered a new approach: by gaining the alliance of Genoa in 1745, the Bourbons were able to circumvent the alpine defences and invade Piedmont from the south. Initial successes, however, were reversed in 1746 and the Austrians and Sardinians won a decisive victory at Piacenza (16 June 1746), ending, for the remainder of the *ancien régime,* a quarter-millennium of French efforts to dominate northern Italy. Later that year, the Austrian alliance invaded Provence, with British naval support, but they were pushed back in 1747, while the Austrians failed to regain Genoa, which had rebelled against their control. The Genoese revolt of December 1746, a successful popular rising, prefigured much that was to be associated with the revolutionary warfare of the close of the century. The swiftly changing course of the conflict in Italy indicated the volatile character of war in this period.

The end of the War of the Austrian Succession with the Peace of Aix-la-Chapelle (1748) left many issues unresolved, particularly Austrian anger over the loss of Silesia. Tension over this led to the outbreak of the Seven Years War in 1756, as Frederick, correctly fearing Austro-Russian plans, launched a pre-emptive strike against Austria's ally, Saxony. Thus began a conflict in which Austria, France, Russia, Saxony and Sweden opposed Frederick, who was allied only to Britain and a small number of German princes. Frederick's survival, the 'miracle of the House of Brandenburg', owed much to impressive victories, especially Rossbach (5 November 1757) over the French, and Leuthen (5 December 1757) and Torgau (3 November 1760) over the Austrians, but also to the failure of his opponents to combine their strategies. After their defeat at Rossbach, the French concentrated on operations against Frederick's allies (British, Hanoverian, Hessian and Brunswicker forces) in Westphalia and Hesse in western Germany, rather than on sending troops east into Saxony to help fight against Frederick himself. The direction of Austrian and Russian advances were different and there was a serious failure to co-operate when Frederick was hard pressed, not least in 1759 after the Russian victory at Kunersdorf (13 August).

OVERLEAF: *Battle of Culloden, 16 April 1746. Decisive defeat of the Jacobites under Charles Edward Stuart by government forces under the Duke of Cumberland. The Jacobites were outnumbered (9,000 to 5,000) and outgunned. The circumstances were not suitable for a Highland charge, not least because Cumberland's numbers permitted defence in depth. Any gaps in the front line could be filled. His artillery, firing canister shot, and infantry so thinned the numbers of the advancing clansmen that those who reached the royal troops were driven back by bayonet.*

There was no equivalent to the partnership of Marlborough and Eugene which had played a major role in winning the War of the Spanish Succession.

Nevertheless, the pressure from Austria and Russia was very strong, and they had no alternative military commitments. Frederick lost control of his Rhenish possessions, and Berlin was raided. The cost of the war to Prussia was very heavy. Frederick's difficulties stemmed in part from recent reforms in the Austrian and Russian armies, not least the development of their artillery; the Austrians had also increased their battlefield flexibility, making successful use of dispersed columns in 1758–9. Furthermore, Frederick was poor at sieges.

Battle of Leuthen, 5 December 1757. Frederick the Great's skilful exploitation of the terrain and the fighting quality of the Prussian army brought victory over a larger Austrian army (54,000 to 35,000) under Prince Charles of Lorraine. The Prussians turned the Austrian position and then defeated the new Austrian front with repeated attacks. The Prussians lost 6,380 killed or wounded, the Austrians 10,000 killed or wounded and 12,000 taken prisoner.

Frederick responded by putting more emphasis on artillery and by adapting his tactics. However, he was unable to exploit battlefield successes and was in any case incapable of striking at the centres of Russian power. He was saved by the death of his most implacable foe, Tsarina Elizabeth, in January 1762, and by the succession of her nephew, Peter III, who treated Frederick as a hero. Once Peter had signed a peace restoring the Russian conquests, the Austrians were left exposed and made peace on the basis of a return to pre-war boundaries.

The British had also contributed to Frederick's victory, both by providing subsidies and by engaging French forces in western Germany. The French were

defeated at Minden (1 August 1759), when British infantry drove their cavalry back. The courage and fire discipline of the British infantry won the battle, six battalions defeating sixty squadrons of French cavalry, by misunderstanding orders, advancing across an open plain and then repulsing two charges by the French cavalry. Most of the cavalry casualties were caused by musket fire, but those who reached the British lines were bayoneted. These charges were followed by a French infantry advance that was stopped by British cannon fire, and then by another French cavalry attack which concentrated on the flanks and rear of the British infantry, only to have the rear ranks turn about and fire their deadly muskets. Again the French charged home, but relatively few reached the British lines and those that did were stopped by the British bayonets. A subsequent infantry attack on the British stopped under cannon fire. The French did not fight well – their planning was poor and their artillery outgunned – but the British cavalry failed to cement the victory by charging. This led to the court-martial of its commander, Lord Sackville. A series of British attacks on the French coasts were less successful. Cherbourg was temporarily seized in 1758 and Belle-Ile off the Breton coast was captured in 1761, but attacks on Rochefort in 1757 and St Malo the following year were less successful.

The war also involved a Franco-Spanish invasion of Portugal in 1762, which was thwarted in part because of the arrival of a British expeditionary force; but it was a campaign with no major engagements. The role played by fortified positions was important, but the difficulties of campaigning in Portugal were more decisive. The mainly Spanish invasion force was hit by sickness, a shortage of supplies, long lines of communication, rain and a lack of knowledge of the terrain.

The Seven Years War established the reputation of the Prussian army and is generally seen as marking the apogee of *ancien régime* warfare. Thereafter, foreign observers flocked to attend Prussian military reviews and the annual manoeuvres in Silesia. Louis-Alexandre Berthier, later Napoleon's chief of staff and minister of war, was much impressed by those he attended in 1783, three years before Frederick's death.

The Prussians demonstrated their continued effectiveness in 1787. A rapidly advancing Prussian army overran the United Provinces in order to establish the authority of the Prince of Orange in the Dutch crisis of that year. The Prussians were helped by the poor quality of the resistance and by the failure of the French to come to the assistance of their Dutch allies. As was customary in western Europe, the absence of an effective defence was crucial to a rapid successful advance. General James Grant noted how much the Prussians under Karl, Duke of Brunswick (1735–1806), a protégé of Frederick the Great, had benefited from the confusion and weakness of the Dutch:

> as he had no train of artillery with him to force the strong passes upon the dikes, and the several very strong fortified places, which they were so good as to abandon without making the smallest resistance.

Brunswick's success left the Prussian reputation high. In 1790 Joseph Ewart, the British envoy in Berlin, wrote:

I have always considered this country as a great machine, composed of above 200,000 men of the best troops in the world, a treasure that would enable it to carry on four or five campaigns ... a more useful ally than any other power.

Yet this army was to succumb to that of Napoleonic France. Brunswick's advance on Paris in 1792 was checked by larger revolutionary forces at Valmy, and the Prussians were defeated at Jena in 1806, only twenty years after Frederick's death. This appears to mark the failure of the *ancien régime* system. There had been mounting criticism of Prussian linear tactics during Frederick's last years. In 1785 Cornwallis had been critical of the lack of flexibility in Prussian tactics and in 1790 a French diplomat wrote of an obvious decline in the Prussian army since Frederick's death.

The Seven Years War should also have established the reputation of the Russians, victors over the Prussians at Gross-Jägersdorf (30 August 1757) and Kunersdorf (12 August 1759), for they demonstrated fighting quality, unit cohesion, discipline and persistence on the battlefield. In their wars with the Turks in 1768–74 and 1787–92, the Russians went on to display flexibility and success. Pre-revolutionary warfare can be dismissed as rigid and anachronistic only if a very narrow view of it is taken.

The variety of warfare at this time is also shown in the conflict between Russian regulars and Polish patriots from 1768, which culminated in the First Partition of Poland in 1772. An attempt by the Russians to suppress Polish independence of action was assisted by the divisions amongst their opponents, but the campaigns were far from easy. The problems of controlling a vast territory were exacerbated by the mobility of the Polish light cavalry, while the decentralized nature of Polish politics ensured that it was not possible to win the war by identifying and capturing a small number of targets. There was an emphasis on mobility; Russian success depended on the remorseless deployment of major resources, as in the successful three-month siege of Cracow in 1772, and on their willingness to force rapidly moving engagements by bold attacks. At Landskron in 1771 Russian infantry and cavalry stormed the Polish position; in the ensuing battle the cavalry put the Polish infantry to flight while the Russian infantry held off the Polish cavalry. At Stalowicz (12 September 1771) a bold, surprise, dawn advance into the village where the forces of Lithuania were based brought the Russians, under Suvorov, victory. More generally, Suvorov's successful emphasis on speed indicated that far from being simply formulaic, as might be suggested by volley training and linear formations, there was a dynamism and flexibility in European warfare of this period.

Infanterie de ligne

CHAPTER SEVEN

THE COMING
OF REVOLUTION

INFANTRY OF THE LINE, 1793–1806, the soldiers who took
Napoleon to victory. From Histoire de l'Empereur Napoleon.

THE COMING OF REVOLUTION

Contemporary etching of an armed sansculotte. The outbreak of war increased the paranoia of French public culture and allowed the Revolutionaries to associate themselves with France. Demonizing their opponents, they waged war by brutalizing subjects and despoiling foreigners in order to produce resources.

As the columns of French citizen-soldiers charged down their opponents in the early 1790s it was easy to see change in effect and to claim that the political revolution in France had caused a military revolution and, indeed, was dependent on the latter for its survival. Yet alongside an awareness of revolutionary change, both in the scale of forces and in the political and social context of warfare, it is necessary to note that the current of change in European armies was already strong, for this helps to explain the numerous military successes of the opponents of revolutionary France. An observer noted of one engagement '[they] advanced in two columns and kept the same order although three six pounders with grape [shot] fired upon them while they scrambled up the rock', but William Leslie was writing not about some advance by the new republican citizen legions of revolutionary France, but about the successful Hessian assault on the fire-power of American-held Fort Washington in November 1776.

The sources of this current of change were varied, but three are worthy of note: first, widespread demographic and economic expansion in Europe from the 1740s; second, the emphasis on the value of reform and the rational approach to problems that characterized the Enlightenment thought; and, third, the impact of the protracted warfare of 1740–62. The first produced the resources for military expansion, the second encouraged an emphasis on novelty, and the third, a period of testing, led to a determination to replace what had been found deficient and to ensure that armies (and societies) were in a better state for future conflicts. The last were seen as likely: in the 1780s, Europe's rulers were not planning for the French Revolutionary War, but they were preparing for major conflicts, such as that which nearly broke out in 1790–91 between the Prussian alliance system and Austria and Russia. Outside Europe, too, there was a process of change, with the increasing adoption of European-style tactics and weaponry in India and the Ottoman empire.

In Europe, Frederick II had considered more flexible tactical ideas in 1768, in

particular an advance in open order; in general, however, there was little change in Prussian methods after the Seven Years War, and in the War of the Bavarian Succession (1778–9) the Prussians were affected by desertion and by the king's less bold generalship. It was in France, humiliated by the armies of Prussia and Britain at Rossbach (1757) and Minden (1759) respectively, that there was the most experimentation in theory and practice and a willingness to challenge the operation, organization, equipment and ethos of the army. In his *Essai général de tactique* (Paris, 1772), Hippolyte de Guibert stressed movement and enveloping manoeuvres, advocated living off the land in order to increase the speed of operations, criticized reliance on fortifications and urged the value of a patriotic

Revolutionary elan: the battle of Lodi, 10 May 1796. The storming of the bridge over the River Adda was important to the French victory, as was Napoleon's able siting of the cannon.

CANNON FIRE

Round shot was fired parallel to the ground. As it bounced forward it still retained sufficient mass and velocity to kill and maim.

TACTICAL FORMATIONS

In his Reflexions Militaires et Politiques *(The Hague, 1735–40), the Marquiz de Santa Cruz, an experienced Spanish general, discussed how best to combine infantry and cavalry.*

citizen army. The concept of the division, a standing unit maintained in peace and war, and including elements of all arms and, therefore, able to operate independently, was developed in France. Such a unit could serve effectively, both as a detached force and as part of a co-ordinated army operating in accordance with a strategic plan. The divisional plan evolved from 1759, and in 1787–8 army administration was arranged along divisional lines.

There was also interest in France in different fighting methods, developing earlier ideas by writers such as Marshal Saxe, whose *Mes rêveries* criticized reliance on fire-power alone, advocating instead a combination of fire-power and shock: 'the insignificancy of small-arms began to be discovered, which makes more noise than they do execution ... I shall appeal to the experience of all mankind, if any single discharge was ever so violent as to disable an enemy from advancing afterwards, to take ample revenge, by pouring in his fire, and at the same instant rushing in with fixed bayonets; it is by this method only, that numbers are to be destroyed, and victories obtained.' Saxe was unhappy with 'the present method of fixing by word of command, as it detains the soldier in a constrained position, prevents his levelling with any exactness'. He preferred individually aimed fire and shock action. Charging with a bayonet was not uncommon in the eighteenth century, but actual hand-to-hand combat with bayonets was rarer. The mere threat by resolute troops was often enough to cause the less resolute to turn and run. Individually aimed fire was more accurate with rifles than muskets. In the latter case, a volley might have greater psychological impact if at close range and followed by a charge.

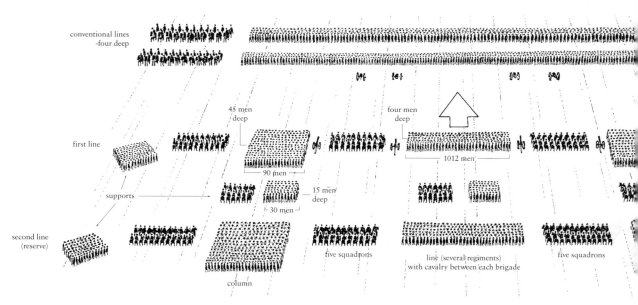

Marshal Saxe was important because he encouraged fresh thoughts about tactics and strategy. He was not alone in this: two other French writers, Jean-Charles Folard and François-Jean de Mesnil-Durand, stressed the shock and weight of force attacking in columns rather than the customary deployment of fire-power and linear tactics. Manoeuvres in 1778 designed to test the rival systems failed to settle the controversy, but the new tactical manual issued in 1791 incorporated both.

The French army was also given better weaponry, in what was increasingly a more important arm of battle, the artillery. Jean-Baptiste Gribeauval (1715–89), who had served during the Seven Years War with the Austrian army, then the best in Europe, standardized the French artillery from 1769, and was appointed inspector-general of artillery in 1776. He used standardized specifications: 4-, 8- and 12-pounder cannon and 6-inch howitzers in eight-gun batteries. Mobility was increased by stronger, larger wheels, shorter barrels and lighter weight cannon, more secure mobile gun carriages and better casting methods. Accuracy was improved by better sights, the issue of gunnery tables and the introduction of inclination markers. The rate of fire rose thanks to the introduction of pre-packaged rounds. Horses were harnessed in pairs instead of in tandem. The theory of war advanced to take note of these changes. In his *De l'usage de l'artillerie nouvelle dans la guerre de campagne* (Paris, 1778), the Chevalier Jean du Teil argued that the artillery should begin battles and should be massed for effect.

Thanks to Gribeauval's reforms, revolutionary France had the best artillery in Europe. In several other respects the army of revolutionary France was a product of pre-revolutionary changes. Napoleon, who had been taught to use Gribeauval's guns, also admired Guibert's work. The regular army was disrupted through desertion and by the emigration of officers, but it played a major role in the successes of 1792, not least because the regulars were better trained than new levies.

Yet the political context of warfare was now very different, not least in providing far larger armies for the French. In August 1793 the revolutionary government ordered general conscription: the entire population could be obliged to serve in the war and all single men between eighteen and twenty-five were to join the army. In 1748 the French under Saxe had overrun the Austrian Netherlands, but only after several years campaigning. In 1792, although the initial attempts to invade the Austrian Netherlands met with disaster, an invasion in November met with overwhelming success and the country fell in a month. The Austrians retook

VOLLEY FIRE

Volley fire relied on a system of ranks in which those who were not firing were refilling their muskets. Under the pressure of battle, it proved difficult to maintain the rate of fire.

15 men deep

30 men

infantry flank guards

OVERLEAF: *The capture of the Dutch fleet, 1795. The benefit of boldness, in this case a cavalry charge across the ice, enabled the French army of the North under General Jean Charles Pichegru to capture the Dutch fleet on the Texel.*

it the following year after their victory at Neerwinden, but by the end of 1794 the French had re-conquered it, as well as driving the Spaniards out of Roussillon and making gains in Catalonia. In the following January, Amsterdam was captured.

Superiority in numbers was important in battles such as Valmy (20 September 1792), Jemappes (6 November 1792), and Wattignies (15–16 October 1793), and in offensives such as that against the Spaniards in Roussillon. Tactics were also important. The characteristic battlefield manoeuvre of French Revolutionary forces, and the most effective way to use the mass of inexperienced soldiers, most of whom went into the infantry, was in independent attack columns. This was also best for an army that put an emphasis on the attack. In contrast, in 1787, Cornwallis had criticized the emphasis on linear formations and rigid drill in the regulations for field exercises drawn up by Sir William Fawcett, the British adjutant general: 'impossible for battalions dressing to their own centres to march together in line. For it often happens, and indeed almost always in action, that the centres cannot see each other. But if they did the least deviation of any leader of a centre from the direction of the march would either enlarge the intervals or throw the battalions upon one another.'

Column advances were far more flexible. At Jemappes the French were able to advance in columns and get back into line at close range, defeating the less numerous Austrians. The French combination of artillery, skirmishers and assault columns was potent, a successful ad hoc combination of tactical elements matched to the technology of the times and the character of the new republican soldier. There was a more 'democratic' command structure, at least at battalion level. The greater dispersal of units ensured that command and co-ordination skills became more important, and the French benefited from young and determined commanders. Those who failed, or were suspected of treachery, were executed. Talent flourished: French commanders included Jean-Baptiste Jourdan, a former private, Lazare Hoche, a former corporal, and Napoleon Bonaparte, initially a junior artillery officer from Corsica, a recent French acquisition.

The armies were systematized by Lazare Carnot, head of the military section of the Committee of Public Safety, who brought a measure of organization to the military confusion. Success in forming and training new armies was instrumental in the transition from a royal army to a nation in arms. The new logistics brought about by the partial abandonment of the magazine system or reliance on fixed depots helped the aggressive style of war – both in strategy and in tactics – of the revolutionary armies, which relied on numbers and enthusiasm. The way was open for the ruthless boldness that Napoleon was to show in Italy in 1796–7. At the same time it is necessary to consider variety, political context and global dimension. Within Europe, the Austrians proved to be tough opponents and the Russians were to show impressive staying power and fighting quality. The politics – military, diplomatic, financial and social – of the Revolution were more important than its tactical innovations. It has been argued that the French soldiers were better motivated and, hence, more successful and better able to use the new methods. This is hard to prove, but, initially at least, revolutionary enthusiasm does seem, by its nature, to have been an important element in French capability. It was probably necessary for the higher morale needed for effective shock action. Patriotic determination was also important to counter the effects of the limited training of the early revolutionary armies.

The failure of French forces to recapture newly independent Haiti in 1802–3 indicated the limited global range of their effectiveness: 40,000 Frenchmen, including Napoleon's brother-in-law, Charles Leclerc, died, the vast majority as a result of yellow fever. The French were driven out by Jean-Jacques Dessalines, who proclaimed himself Emperor Jacques I. This lesser-known imperial counterpart of Napoleon indicated that in Haiti, as elsewhere, the successful use of force was crucial to power.

The storming of Seringapatam, 4 May 1799. The capital of Tipu Sultan of Mysore was a formidable position on an island in the River Cauvery, and George Harris had to succeed before the monsoon swelled the river. The artillery on the opposite bank blew a breach in the ramparts, and this was stormed under heavy fire. Part of the British force was held in savage fighting until the defenders were outflanked by the British troops who had gained the inner rampart and then moved along. The defenders were thrown into disorder and slaughtered with heavy losses, including Tipu.

Battle of Valmy, 20 September 1792. Far from being the triumph of a new military order, this was not a full-scale battle. The outnumbered Prussians were checked by the strength of the French position, especially the artillery, which came from the ancien régime *army, and retreated.*

CONCLUSION

THE WORLD PICTURE

THE RUSSIANS CLEAR THE UPPER DNIESTER, 1769. *Prince Aleksandr Golitsyn captured the major fortress of Khotin, but he had been less than impressive and was replaced by Rumyantsev who was to inflict serious defeats on the Turks the following year. Fortresses played a major role in the Russo-Turkish war of 1768–74.*

CONCLUSION: THE WORLD PICTURE

THE EIGHTEENTH CENTURY prior to the French Revolution is commonly regarded as a period of military conservatism, indecisiveness and stagnation, part of an interlude between periods of 'military revolution' in 1560–1660 and 1792–1815. It may possibly be more helpful to think neither of revolution nor of revolutions, certainly between the early sixteenth-century deployment of gunpowder weaponry in long-range warships and on the battlefield, and the sweeping organizational and technological changes of the nineteenth century. But that does not imply that warfare in the meantime was static. Armies and fleets competed for major goals. The fate of North America was settled, as was the struggle between Britain and France in India. French hegemony in western Europe was resisted, the Turks were pushed back from much of Europe, and the Chinese greatly extended their power over non-Chinese peoples. Elsewhere, war led to the rise of other powers, such as Afghanistan under the Durranis, Burma under Alaung-hpaya, and Gurkha Nepal; and the collapse of others, such as Safavid Persia and Mughal India. War was central to the history of the period and to the experience of its peoples, and these wars were far from inconsequential.

British success over France ensured that North America would have a political culture derived from Britain. A French-dominated transoceanic world would have looked to Catholicism, civil law, French culture and language, and a different notion of representative government and politics to that of Britain. Thus, the eighteenth century was important not only to the rise of the West but also to the question, 'which West?'. The result was not inevitable. If in 1815 Britain was the strongest state in the world, the situation had been ver different seventy years earlier, as Jacobite forces under Bonnie Prince Charlie advanced on Derby, outmanoueuvring the armies sent to defeat them,

Civil conflict. The deterioration in relations between William V of Orange and the Patriots led to civil conflict in the United Provinces (modern Netherlands) and, eventually, in 1787, to a successful invasion on behalf of William V by a Prussian army. Patriot forces proved far less effective than their American counterparts.

A BRITISH FERGUSON
RIFLE

*This weapon used a
screw-down breech plug
shown here in the open
position. The rifle barrel
offered greater accuracy
than the mass-produced
musket, but was more
expensive to produce and
did not carry a bayonet.*

while the British government feared a supporting French invasion of southern
England. If by 1815 Britain was the dominant military power in India, in 1746 the
British had lost Madras to the French. There was nothing inevitable in the British
triumph. Indeed, a Jacobite triumph in 1745–6 would have altered Britain's
position in the world, and the character of the 'West', not only with regard to
political alignments but also with reference to the nature of public culture,
economic interest and social dynamics.

Apart from these grand shifts – of territorial
change and state-building – armies were also
responsible for the maintenance of order and the
defence of authority around the world, whether
against brigands or against striking workers, since
most states had no equivalent to a national police
force. Order was imposed by the army both within
states, for example in tumultuous cities such as
Madrid in 1766 and London in 1780, and in unruly
borderlands, where smugglers and other defiers of
authority flourished. An Indian commentator, Dean
Mahomet, recorded in 1772:

> we perceived that Captain Brooke, a very
> active officer, at the head of five companies of
> sepoys ... had been, some time, engaged in the
> pursuit of the Pahareas, a savage clan that
> inhabit the mountains between Bohogolpore
> and Rajmahal, and annoy the peaceable
> resident and unwary traveller: numbers,
> happily were taken ... some severely whipped
> in a public manner; and, others ... suspended
> on a kind of gibbet, ignominiously exposed
> along the mountain's conspicuous brow, in
> order to strike terror into the hearts of their
> accomplices.

The need to maintain order was not a task only
placed on European and European-commanded forces.
The Turkish army, for example, suppressed risings
both in the capital, Constantinople, and in the

provinces, such as Egypt. Furthermore, the Turkish army was used in borderlands, against, for example, the Bedouin. Similarly, the Chinese army acted against risings, both by Chinese, for example the White Lotus rebellion of 1796–1805 in Shensi, and by non-Chinese subjects, such as the Chin-Ch'uan tribal rising in Szechwan in 1746–9 and the Yo tribal rising in Kwangsi in 1790.

Reference to Afghanistan, Burma, China and Nepal serves as a reminder of the weaknesses of the Eurocentric perspective. Warfare in much of the world was planned and waged without reference to European weaponry, methods or politics. The Europeans made a major impact in India and Sri Lanka, but elsewhere in south Asia this was definitely not the case, and even less so in east Asia. There the advance that had taken European power to the Philippines,

The eighteenth-century 'Military–Industrial Complex'. Metallurgical industries developed in part to meet the growing demand for armaments, especially cannon. This was particularly true of the Russian iron industry in the Urals, and of British ironworks, for example, this one in Shropshire.

Formosa (Taiwan), Siberia's Pacific coast and the Amur Valley had already been partially reversed, the Dutch being driven from Formosa in 1661 and the Russians from the Amur Valley in the 1680s. There was no resumption of the pace of European advance in this region in the eighteenth century. It is not necessary to explain this by reference to any supposed failure of the European military system; the European powers concentrated first on war with each other in Europe itself and, second, on attacks on other European colonial possessions.

Conflict with non-European powers, particularly those that were not close neighbours, came a long way behind. It was important, however, in that it measured the relative military and political prowess of European powers in the global theatre, and their adaptability to radically different situations. Also, such as the wars between the armies and navies of European powers, conflicts with non-Europeans were forcing houses for tactical innovations and weapons developments that informed warfare throughout the world in the nineteenth and twentieth centuries.

Europe became the major innovator of weapons and methods, and European military and political power would eventually dominate the world. This owed much to the greater, or possibly different, ambition of European nations, indicated in part by the failure of sophisticated east and south Asian states to develop oceanic naval power. Indigenous peoples and states outside Europe, when confronted by European aggression, had two advantages: first, superior numbers locally and second, greater knowledge of, cultural identity with and administrative control over local territory. European success can be explained by a variety and varying combination of factors, and the way in which the combination held or was held together was in itself important: for example, the British East India Company was, despite its frequent internal disputes, a corporation of seamless continuity and was competing with personalized autocracies which were dependent on strong leadership and which were vulnerable to recurrent succession crises. More generally, the Europeans benefited from the post-feudal, non-personalized nature of their military command systems and command philosophy, especially the application of reason and science to command problems. The same was equally true of weapons development and tactical theory, which, since the Renaissance, were far more highly developed in Europe. The number of manuals and speculative works on warfare seems to have been far greater there than elsewhere, and this helped change aspects of warfare that were hidebound, instinctive and traditional. Scientific developments

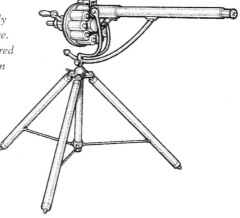

PUCKLE'S GUN, 1718

Puckle's gun was an early attempt at automatic fire. It is supposed to have fired sixty-three shots in seven minutes.

were utilized. In 1788 Dr Charles Blagden described the French harbour works at Cherbourg as 'a new experiment in mechanics'.

In 1776 the Scottish economist Adam Smith offered, in his *Inquiry into the Nature and Causes of the Wealth of Nations*, an analysis of the sociology of warfare, in which he contrasted nations of hunters, shepherds and husbandmen with the 'more advanced state of society', in which industry was important. These advanced societies were seen as providing a hierarchy of military organization and sophistication in which 'a well-regulated standing army' was vital to the defence of civilization. Firearms, Smith argued, were crucial in the onset of military modernity:

A LIGHT REGIMENTAL GUN

A light regimental gun. c. 1755. This Swiss example fired a two-pound ball.

> Before the invention of fire-arms, that army was superior in which the soldiers had, each individually, the greatest skill in dexterity in the use of their arms ... since the invention ... strength and agility of body, or even extraordinary dexterity and skill in the use of arms, though they are far from being of no consequence, are, however, of less consequence ... In modern war the great expence of fire-arms gives an evident advantage to the nation which can best afford that expence; and consequently, to an opulent and civilized, over a poor and barbarous nation. In ancient times the opulent and civilized found it difficult to defend themselves against the poor and barbarous nations. In modern times the poor and barbarous find it difficult to defend themselves against the opulent and civilized.

Smith exaggerated the military advantages of the 'opulent and civilized', but he captured an important shift. Those he termed 'civilized' were no longer on the defensive. This had been unclear in the first half of the century: Peter the Great had been defeated at the Pruth (1711); the Dsungars had overrun Tibet (1717) and the Afghans Persia (1722–3); the Russians had been forced to abandon Persia (1732) and the Austrians to surrender Belgrade and northern Serbia to the Turks (1739).

The nature of each of these episodes can be qualified, and the relationship between military development and civilization questioned; were, for example, the Turks less civilized than the Austrians or the Persians than the Russians? Nevertheless, however defined, there is no doubting that a major shift occurred in Eurasia. By 1760 in east Asia and 1770 in eastern Europe, the land forces of China and the Europeans respectively were able to see off attacks by more primitively organized and less well armed adversaries, and between 1750 and 1792 their land frontiers were pushed outward. Political and economic relations changed with this military shift. In the New World and Africa there was no

OVERLEAF: *The storming of Ochakov, 1788. This major Turkish fortress on the shores of the Black Sea was besieged by Catherine the Great's favourite, Prince Potemkin, in June 1788, but limited success forced him to resort to storming the ramparts that December. This was successful, but the need to adopt this tactic was a comment on the limitations of Russian siegecraft.*

comparable shift as, in both, the trends of the previous century were maintained: advancing frontiers of control and settlement in the New World and no real changes in the situation between Europeans and non-Europeans in Africa. In Australasia, however, the arrival of European forces in 1788 was followed by the rapid establishment of a new military and political order. The Aborigines were not in a position to mount sustained resistance in areas where the environment encouraged large numbers of European settlers: they lacked numbers, fire-power and large-scale organization, and were being exposed to new diseases. In contrast, the Dutch expedition sent in 1696–7 to explore the west coast of Australia had reported that the 'southland' offered little for the Dutch East India Company, and the Dutch had not established a base.

In south Asia the situation was more complex. If forces such as those of Nadir Shah and the Afghans are defined as barbarous, i.e. less sophisticated, then their invasions of India can be seen as a defeat for the civilized, and this spurred on the process of military change. India was certainly an area of rapid changes in weaponry and military organization; European-style infantry forces were created by, for example, the Marathas and the Nizam of Hyderabad. A volatile and pressurized international system was driving the pace of military adaptability. French experts taught Indians to cast cannon in the French style and also played a role in local fortification technique. Thus, Benoît de Boigne, commander of a corps for the Maratha leader Sindhia, constructed French-style fortifications in Aligarh, east of Delhi, after 1788. Indian rulers could deploy considerable forces. In 1781 John Bristow, the British Resident in Lucknow, estimated that the forces of the Mughal emperor, not generally noted then as a military power, included thirty battalions of sepoys and 5,000 rocket men, all paid by the Mughals, and 73,000 infantry and cavalry supplied by dependent lords.

In hindsight such forces seem obsolete, foredoomed to defeat by the British because of deficient weaponry and organization. When in the 1750s and 1760s many Indian mercenary troops came into the service of the British East India Company with their own weapons, the company officers considered them to be nearly worthless. In 1754 the 39th Foot became the first substantial unit of the British army to reach India. Seven years later, John Carnac, an officer in the East India Company's Bengal army, who had just defeated a Mughal force, argued that it was foolish to have European cavalry in the company's army: 'nor will our establishment of Europeans admit of their being otherwise employed than as infantry, in which alone our immense superiority over the country [Indian] powers will always consist'. In 1782 Sir John Burgoyne wrote from Madras, 'Your Lordship would not believe your eyes if you saw an Indian battalion move; the number of attendants, servants, bullocks, palanquins etc. astonished me beyond measure, and it's absolutely impossible any army with one quarter of such incumbrances can move at all.'

Five years later, Captain William Kirkpatrick, British Resident at Sindhia's court, reported unsympathetically from Agra about the latter's attempts to train infantry and artillery along European lines. He noted the appointment of Europeans:

> to form a body of troops upon the model of one of our brigades ... They have together under them about 125 men whom they call Europeans; but these chiefly consist of Armenians, and the Black Christians usually though improperly called Portuguese. Each of those, I understand, is to have the command of a gun. Including calibres of all sizes, Shinde's train of artillery consists of about 200 pieces. A few of these are very good guns; but in general they are contemptible. The number of tumbrils belonging to his [artillery] park is inconsiderable; the ammunition being for the most part transported in common hackeries ... Were he opposed to an active enemy, it would almost to a certainty bring about his ruin.

Indeed, in 1798–1816 the British defeated Mysore, the Marathas and the Gurkhas and forced the Nizam to disband his French-officered force. However such successes appeared far from obvious in 1779–83, when the British were hard pressed by the Marathas and Mysore, whose forces were certainly mobile. Campaigning against Tipu Sultan of Mysore, Cornwallis wrote from his camp in December 1791, 'The expectations entertained in England of our success have been too sanguine ... it is no easy task to provide for the subsistence of vast multitudes in a distant desert, nor can it be the work of a day to subdue a Prince so active and capable and possessed of such immense reserves, and so well served by his officers.' A British observer in 1791 described 'their infantry in regular files, with guns in the intervals, drawn by long teams of large bullocks as white as milk'.

Kirkpatrick was overly harsh. Sindhia's army proved successful in campaigns in Rajputana in the 1780s and 1790s, and his artillery captured the major Rajput fortress of Chitor in a matter of weeks. Sindhia's forces were eventually to be defeated by the British under Arthur Wellesley, later Duke of Wellington, in 1803, but it is important to be cautious about viewing Indian states, as Kirkpatrick did, as 'less advanced in political and military knowledge'. There was no clear basis for any system of ranking and any suggestion of determinism has to be queried.

It may seem unsatisfactory to end on a note of caution and a long way from the battlefields of Napoleonic Europe. But this is deliberate. The relationship between European and non-European forces and methods of warfare was the crucial 'story' in the military history of the eighteenth century. As Napoleon fought his way across northern Italy in 1796–7, it was still far from clear that Britain would be able to dominate India or defeat the French challenge to British naval predominance, and British control over Ireland, or prevent the French establishing their power along the route to India. War served many ends. There was still everything to fight for.

SOME LEADING COMMANDERS

AMHERST, JEFFREY, 1ST LORD (1717–97)
British commander-in-chief of the army 1772–95.
Successful as commander in Canada in last stages
of Seven Years War, but less effective as
administrator.

ANSON, GEORGE, LORD (1697–1762)
British admiral who successfully attacked Spaniards
on circumnavigation of world in 1740–4, beat
French off Cape Finisterre in 1747, and became an
effective First Lord of the Admiralty.

AUGUSTUS II OF SAXONY, KING OF POLAND
(1670–1733)
Heavily beaten by Charles XII of Sweden in Great
Northern War, losing a series of engagements in
1700–7.

BELLE ISLE, CHARLES, DUKE OF (1684–1761)
Bellicose French general who fought in Wars of
Polish and Austrian Succession and sought reform as
Minister of War 1757–60.

BERWICK, JAMES, DUKE OF (1670–1734)
Illegitimate son of James II and nephew of Duke of
Marlborough. Fought well in War of the Spanish
Succession, winning at Almanza (1707). Invaded
Spain again in 1719. Killed by cannon ball at siege
of Philippsburg, 1734.

BROGLIE, VICTOR, DUKE OF (1718–1804)
Major French general in Seven Years War, he helped
introduce the divisional structure.

BRUNSWICK, KARL, DUKE OF (1735–1806)
Major Prussian general who successfully invaded
United Provinces (Netherlands) in 1787, but was
checked by Revolutionary French at Valmy in 1792.
Mortally wounded by Napoleon's forces at battle of
Auerstadt.

CARNOT, LAZARE (1753–1823)
Engineer officer, who played crucial role in
organizing French war effort in 1793–4. A master of
expedients, he raised new armies, and was partly
responsible for the victories of 1794.

CHARLES V OF LORRAINE, PRINCE (1712–80)
Brother-in-law of Maria Theresa of Austria, he
played a leading role in the War of the Austrian
Succession, being beaten several times by Frederick
the Great, including at Hohenfriedburg (1745) and
Soor (1745). In the Seven Years War, beaten by
Frederick at Prague (1757) and badly defeated at
Leuthen (1757).

CHARLES XII, KING OF SWEDEN (1682–1718)
Energetic general who was largely responsible
for the Swedes doing so well for so long in Great
Northern War. Defeated Russians at Narva in 1700
and repeatedly beat Saxons in Poland, but
decisively defeated by Peter the Great at Poltava in
1709.

CLIVE, ROBERT, 1ST LORD (1725–74)
Thwarted French plans in India and defeated greatly
more numerous army of Nawab of Bengal at Plassey
(1757).

CORNWALLIS, CHARLES, MARQUESS (1738–1805)
Forced to surrender at besieged Yorktown (1781) by
George Washington, Cornwallis was more
successful against Tipu Sultan of Mysore in 1792
and in Ireland in 1798.

CUMBERLAND, WILLIAM, DUKE OF (1721–65)
Second surviving son of George II of Britain, he was
defeated by the French under Saxe at Fontenoy
(1745), but crushed the Jacobites at Culloden
(1746). Unsuccessfully defended Hanover against
French in 1757.

DAUN, LEOPOLD, COUNT (1705–66)
Austrian opponent of Frederick the Great he defeated him at Kolin (1757) and fought well at Torgau (1760). A master of position warfare, he was more effective than Charles of Lorraine.

EUGENE, PRINCE (1663–1736)
Thwarted of patronage in France, Eugene fled to serve Austria. He did so with great effect against the Turks, especially at Zenta (1697), Peterwardein (1716) and Belgrade (1717), and the French, particularly at Turin (1706) and, in co-operation with Marlborough, at Blenheim (1704), Oudenaarde (1708) and Malplaquet (1709). A flexible master of war.

FERDINAND OF BRUNSWICK, DUKE (1721–92)
An able opponent of France who served Frederick the Great. Defeated French at Minden (1759) and protected Frederick's western flank during Seven Years War.

FREDERICK II, THE GREAT, KING OF PRUSSIA (1719–86)
A master tactician and fine strategist, Frederick defeated the Austrians and French, but found the Russians a more formidable foe. Ready to take risks with the proficient Prussian army he inherited. His victories at Rossbach and Leuthen in 1757 were his masterpieces.

GALWAY, HENRY, EARL OF (1648–1720)
Huguenot (French Protestant) who commanded English forces in Spain and was defeated at Almanza (1707).

GREENE, NATHANAEL (1742–86)
One of the more effective American commanders, Greene was sent to command in the south in 1780. Although defeated at Guilford Courthouse (1781), Greene's pressure on Cornwallis contributed to the British failure in the south.

GRIBEAUVAL, JEAN BAPTISTE (1715–89)
Helped to standardize French field artillery and

made it particularly effective. Napoleon was the prime beneficiary.

HOCHE, LOUIS LAZARE (1768–97)
A corporal before the French Revolution, Hoche became a general in 1793 and that year pushed the Austrians and Prussians back across the Rhine. Suppressed the Royalist Chouans in Brittany.

HOWE, WILLIAM, VISCOUNT (1729–1814)
Commander of the British forces in North America in 1776–8, Howe took New York and Philadelphia, but failed to destroy Washington.

KOSCIUSZKO, TADEUSZ (1746–1817)
Polish soldier who served the American Revolutionaries as an engineer. Fought Russians in Poland in 1792 and 1794. Defended Warsaw effectively in 1794, but defeated and captured at Maciejowice.

LACY, FRANZ, COUNT (1725–1801)
Important commander in Austrian army who served against Frederick the Great in Seven Years War and in Turkish war of 1788–91.

LOUDON, GIDEON, FREIHERR VON (1717–90)
Major Austrian general in Seven Years War who co-operated with Russians to defeat Frederick the Great at Kunersdorf (1759).

MARLBOROUGH, JOHN CHURCHILL, 1ST DUKE OF (1650–1722)
Masterly British general who played key role in thwarting French during War of the Spanish Succession. Victorious at Blenheim (1704), Ramillies (1706) and Oudenaarde (1708), but his last major victory at Malplaquet (1709) was very costly. Master tactician.

MERCY, CLAUDIUS, COUNT OF (1666–1734)
An able cavalry commander and protégé of Eugene who helped him defeat the Turks in 1716–18. Killed

at the battle of Parma trying to drive the French from northern Italy.

MÜNNICH, BURKHARD, COUNT OF (1683–1767)
German in Russian service, who successfully commanded invasion of Poland in 1733 and played a major role in war with Turks in 1736–9.

NADIR SHAH, SHAH OF PERSIA (1688–1747)
Spent much of his reign at war with Turkey, but also invaded India in 1739, defeating the Mughals at Karnal and occupying Delhi. Also expanded into Central Asia, and, less successfully, attacked Georgia and Oman.

PETER THE GREAT (1672–1725)
A bellicose ruler of Russia who fought the Turks and Sweden. Captured Azov from Turks in 1696, but defeated by them at the Pruth in 1711. Beaten by Charles XII of Sweden at Narva in 1700, but smashed his forces at Poltava (1709) and went on to conquer Sweden's eastern Baltic provinces. Modernized Russian army.

PONTIAC (C. 1720–69)
Chief of the Ottawa tribe, he led resistance to the British in North America in 1763–4. Captured many forts in 1763, but forced to agree to a truce in 1765.

POTEMKIN, GREGORY, PRINCE (1731–91)
Lover and adviser of Catherine the Great, commanded against Turks in 1787–91. Depended heavily on ability of Suvorov.

RAMA I (d. 1809)
Chakri, Siamese general who seized throne in 1782. Fought off Burmese attacks in 1785 and 1786.

RODNEY, GEORGE, LORD (1718–92)
British admiral who did well in the West Indies in 1762, and defeated the French at the battle of the Saints in 1782.

SAXE, HERMANN, COUNT OF (1696–1750)
Illegitimate son of Elector of Saxony who made a brilliant career in French service, defeating Allied forces in 1745–8, especially at Fontenoy (1745). Also wrote on war.

STUART, CHARLES EDWARD (1720–88)
'Bonnie Prince Charlie' invaded Scotland successfully in 1745, winning victory at Prestonpans, but his invasion of England was abandoned at Derby, and he was crushed at Culloden (1746).

SUVOROV, ALEXANDER (1729–1800)
Russian Field Marshal, who was especially successful against the Turks in 1787–92 and against the French in north Italy in 1799. A vigorous master of the offensive.

TIPU SULTAN (1749–99)
Ruler of Mysore from 1782, he fought the British, but was defeated in 1792, and killed when his capital Seringapatam was stormed.

VILLARS, CLAUDE (1653–1734)
Effective French general who made Marlborough's victory at Malplaquet (1709) very costly. Invaded northern Italy successfully in 1733–4.

WASHINGTON, GEORGE (1732–99)
Creator of the Continental Army of the American Revolution, Washington was not a brilliant tactician, as defeats at Long Island (1776) and Brandywine (1777) showed, but he learned from his mistakes, was an effective leader, and forced the British to surrender at Yorktown (1781).

WOLFE, JAMES (1727–59)
Brilliantly successful in winning victory outside Québec in 1759, Wolfe died at his moment of triumph.

FURTHER READING

The major problem with the literature on the period is its Eurocentricity. A different approach is taken by J. M. Black, *War and the World 1450–2000* (New Haven, 1998) and Black (ed.), *War in the Early Modern World 1450–1815* (London, 1999). See also Douglas Peers (ed.), *Warfare and Empires: Contact and Conflict between European and Non-European Military and Maritime Forces and Cultures* (Aldershot, 1997). For China, T. J. Barfield, *The Perilous Frontier: Nomadic Empires and China* (Oxford, 1989). For India, J. J. L. Gommans, *The Rise of the Indo-Afghan Empire, c. 1710–1780* (Leiden, 1995) and D. H. A. Kolff, *Naukar, Rajput and Sepoy: The Ethnohistory of the Military Labour Market in Hindustan 1450–1850* (Cambridge, 1990). For the East Indies, M. C. Ricklefs, *War, Culture and Economy in Java, 1677–1726* (The Hague, 1990). For the Balkans, V .J. Parry and M. E. Yapp (eds), *War, Technology and Society in the Middle East* (Oxford, 1975).

For Africa, R. A. Smith, *Warfare and Diplomacy in Pre-Colonial West Africa* (2nd edn, Madison, 1989), J. F. Searing, *West African Slavery and Atlantic Commerce. The Senegal River Valley, 1700–1860* (Cambridge, 1993), John Thornton, *Warfare in Atlantic Africa, 1500–1800* (London, 1999), R. A. Kea, 'Firearms and Warfare on the Gold and Slave Coasts from the Sixteenth to the Nineteenth Centuries', *Journal of African History* (1971), W. Richards, 'The Import of Firearms into West Africa', *Journal of African History* (1980), and several works by Robin Law: *The Oyo Empire c.1600–c.1836: a West African Imperialism in the Era of Atlantic Slave Trade* (Oxford, 1977), *The Horse in West African History* (London, 1980), 'Warfare on the West African Slave Coast, 1650–1850', in R. B. Ferguson and N. L. Whitehead (eds.), *War in the Tribal Zone: Expanding States and Indigenous Warfare* (Santa Fé, 1992) and '"Here is No Resisting the Country". The Realities of Power in Afro-European Relations on the West African "Slave Coast"', *Itinerario* (1994).

For North America, C. Calloway, *The Western Abenakis of Vermont, 1600–1800* (Norman, Oklahoma, 1990), D. Ritcher, *The Ordeal of the Longhouse: Peoples of the Iroquois League in the Era of European Colonization* (Chapel Hill, 1992), Armstrong Starkey, *European and Native American Warfare 1675–1815* (London, 1998) and Ian K. Steele, *Warpaths. Invasions of North America* (Oxford, 1994).

On South America, J. Hemming, *Red Gold: The Conquest of the Brazilian Indians, 1500–1760* (2nd edn, London, 1995) and O. Cornblit, *Power and Violence in a Colonial City: Oruro from the Mining Renaissance to the Rebellion of Túpac Amaru, 1740–1782* (Cambridge, 1995). For a detailed account of successful resistance, D. Sweet, 'Native resistance in eighteenth-century Amazonia: the "Abominable Muras" in War and Peace', *Radical History Review* (1992).

Naval history and warfare can be approached through Jan Glete, *Navies and Nations. Warships, Navies and State Building in Europe and America, 1500–1860* (Stockholm, 1993), Richard Harding, *Seapower and Naval Warfare 1650–1830* (London, 1999), and J. R. Bruijn, *The Dutch Navy of the Seventeenth and Eighteenth Centuries* (Columbia, South Carolina, 1993). For colonial warfare through J. R. McNeill, *Atlantic Empires of France and Spain: Havana and Louisbourg, 1700–1763* (Chapel Hill, 1985) and J. M. Black, *Britain as a Military Power 1688–1815* (London, 1999). The landward extension of European empire in Central Asia can be approached through A. S. Donnelly, *The Russian Conquest of Bashkiria, 1552–1740* (New Haven, 1968) and M. Khodarkovsky, *Where Two Worlds Met: The Russian State and the Kalmyck Nomads 1600–1771* (Ithaca, 1771). For North America, David Weber, *The Spanish Frontier in North America* (New Haven, 1992).

For the European colonies in North America, Fred Anderson, *A People's Army. Massachusetts Soldiers and Society in the Seven Years' War* (Chapel Hill, 1984) and Christon Archer, *The Army in Bourbon Mexico 1760–1810* (Albuquerque, 1977). For the American War of Independence, J. M. Black, *War for America* (Stroud, 1991) and Harry Ward, *The War for Independence and the Transformation of American Society* (London, 1999).

On Europe see, most recently, J. M. Black (ed.), *European Warfare 1453–1815* (London, 1999). For earlier introductory work, John Childs, *Armies and Warfare in Europe 1648–1789* (Manchester, 1982), Russell Weigley, *The Age of Battles. The Quest for Decisive Warfare from Breitenfeld to Waterloo* (Bloomington, 1991), and J. M. Black, *European Warfare 1660–1815* (New Haven, 1994). For the beginning of the century, David Chandler, *The Art of War in the Age of Marlborough* (London, 1975) and John Lynn, *Giant of the Grand Siècle. The French Army 1610–1715* (Cambridge, 1997). For mid century, Christopher Duffy, *Frederick the Great. A Military Life* (London, 1985) and *The Military Experience in the Age of Reason* (2nd edn., London, 1998), and Dennis Showalter, *The Wars of Frederick the Great* (London, 1996). For the 1790s, Gunther Rothenberg, *The Art of Warfare in the Age of Napoleon* (London, 1977), T. C. W. Blanning, *The French Revolutionary Wars 1787–1802* (London, 1996), and W. S. Cormack, *Revolution and New Political Conflict in the French Navy 1789–1794* (Cambridge, 1995), and, on the global scale, C. A. Bayly, *Imperial Meridian. The British Empire and the World 1780–1830* (Harlow, 1989). On Russia, Duffy, *Russia's Military Way to the West. Origins and Nature of Russian Military Power 1700–1800* (London, 1981), and W. C. Fuller, *Strategy and Power in Russia 1660–1914* (New York, 1992). On Germany, Peter Wilson, *War and German Politics 1648–1806* (London, 1998). On siegecraft, Duffy, *The Fortress in the Age of Vauban and Frederick the Great, 1660–1789* (London, 1985). More generally on the causes of war see J. M. Black, *Why Wars Happen* (London, 1998). The quantity of first-rate work on warfare in Europe sits uneasily with the very different situation for regions such as Ethiopia, Persia and Indo-China.

INDEX

PICTURE CREDITS

E. T. Archive Endpapers and pp. 2–3, 6, 22–3, 25, 26, 27, 38, 39, 42–3, 47, 49, 50, 54, 74, 79, 83, 87, 88, 89, 101, 105, 124, 128, 131, 134–5, 144–5, 146 , 150–51, 154, 160–61, 165, 168–9, 180–81, 192–3, 200–201, 207. A.K.G. Front jacket and pp. 14, 16–17, 18–19, 51, 60, 61, 64–5, 68, 82, 86, 90–91, 120, 157, 158, 167, 174, 192, 202, 204–205, 210–11. Peter Newark Pictures Jacket flap and pp. 20, 22, 58, 78, 94, 108–109, 119, 125, 138, 142–3, 149, 156, 159, 162, 168, 171, 175. Barnaby's/Fotomas Index pp. 24, 29, 30, 31, 32, 48–9, 56, 66, 70–71, 76, 97, 98–9, 130, 136–7, 141, 153, 172, 179, 184–5, 186–7, 190, 198, 212. Royal Armoury pp 57, 103. Werner Forman Archive pp 57, 103. Corbis pp. 70, 110, 116, 122, 123. Mary Evans Picture Library pp. 102, 112–13, 114–15, 152, 196–7.

Drawings on the title page and on pages 79, 118, 159, 166, 167, 182, 194, 195, 206, 208 and 209 are by Peter Smith and Malcolm Swanston of Arcadia Editions Ltd

ENDPAPER: *Battle of Fontenoy, 11 May 1745, by Philippoteaux. Lt. Col. Lord Charles Hay, commanding the First Foot Guards, walks out between the lines and drinks a toast, shouting a taunt before saluting the French Guards facing him. Moments later, with a tremendous volley, the English advance resumed, smashing through the first French line. Saxe, although suffering from dropsy, roused himself from the litter on which he had been carried and established a second line which, in an exchange of firing, halted the English attack.*

In 1757 Alaung-hpaya stormed Pegu, uniting Burma under his rule. In the same year Frederick the Great of Prussia, fighting in what came to be known as the Seven Years War, defeated his French and Austrian opponents at Rossbach and Leuthen respectively. Both were important campaigns in the history of eighteenth-century warfare. Both are covered in this important and wide-ranging narrative by a leading authority in early modern warfare, which presents a full and fascinating picture of war both in Europe and elsewhere in the world at this time.

In eighteenth-century Europe warfare was widespread. Armies fought with flintlocks and bayonets, and in conflicts such as the Wars of European Succession and the Seven Years War success generally lay in speed and decisiveness. The tactical innovations of European leaders such as Marlborough and Frederick the Great made them figures who are still renowned today.

Yet the most successful military power in the world at the time was not European but Chinese, the largest land battles of the century occurring not in Prussia but in India. In 1717 Dsungar horsemen invaded Tibet and began the expansion of China to its greatest ever geographical extent. Between 1725 and 1745 the Afghan leader Nadir Shah invaded Persia and India using cavalry and camel-mounted swivel guns. And on the North American frontiers Native Americans were defeated through the settlers' economic superiority and weight of numbers.

In this refreshingly non-Eurocentric book, Jeremy Black examines warfare on a global scale at a time when the face of war was beginning to change. He describes new technology, from the introduction of the socket bayonet to the invention of the elevating screw for cannon. He covers innovations such as the guerrilla tactics that defeated the British in the American War of Independence. And he describes in detail the changes in ideology that led to the French Revolution, a conflict that was to have effects lasting well into the next century.